An Inquiry Into Human Motivation

By

Bert Nemcik

Lifelong Learning Network

Table of Contents

1. AN INQUIRY INTO MOTIVATION IN HUMAN BEINGS

Motivation is the force that initiates, directs, and sustains individual or group behavior in order to satisfy a need or to attain a goal. This force is unique to each individual human being. There are many forces that drive an individual to struggle to achieve a goal or to fulfill a need. What are some of these?

Some individuals born into squalor strive their entire lives to escape their birthright. They often sacrifice their health, their safety and their very existence to succeed. What is it that motivates them?

Our nation developed because many individuals risked everything to reach beyond what "was" to what "could be." Settlers in the East cut native timbers in order to expose the earth to the sun above and sowed crops upon the rocky soil of the East. Homesteaders endured great hardships crossing the Great Plains to establish homesteads, ranches, and business in the Wild West. Many died in the process of making a new life for themselves. Their names are unknown to us, and yet in many of us, the same rugged individualism still exists and motivates us to struggle toward similar, contemporary pursuits.

Some people are intrinsically motivated to achieve their goals or to satisfy needs. They do what they do just for the joy of doing it. There are no external factors that drive them. You and I have known such individuals and sometimes they can appear to be a mystery to us unless we understand their internal drive to succeed at what they are doing.

Opposite of the intrinsically motivated individual is she who is extrinsically motivated to achieve something. Her behaviors are easier to understand. Take for example a woman that after years of working at a minimum wage job, decides to develop new skills in order to qualify for a better position. She sacrifices time and energy to achieve her goal. She becomes a nurse, a teacher, a business woman, and in her new labor, earns the money she so desired.

Some people are personally invested in improving themselves. They possess a value system which forces them to step beyond their status quo and improve their condition in life. The values that drive them may be simple or complex depending upon cultural and other environmental factors. If a person values money above all else, he or she will succeed in amassing the wealth desired. This "American Dream" was certainly active in the 1950's when many millionaires were born, rising out of the ruins like the phoenix from the aftermath of WWII.

Personal investment aids the individual in motivating himself to succeed in life. In viewing life from a personal perspective, the individual makes decisions which will foster the kinds of successes he desires. Investing in self was a predominant theme in the late 1970's and 1980's. Many individuals, unlike their predecessors in the 1960's, invested in the bull markets and gathered fame and fortune. This motivating factor is present in all humans to some degree.

In some individuals there is a self-determination which motivates stellar performance. The determination to be something other than what one is is the force that motivates this kind of individual to attain success. The self-determined individual is more likely to succeed at what he wants to because within him exists this force which prompts him to continue to struggle regardless of the barriers confronting him.

Freud (1939) hypothesized that all individuals possess drives which cause individuals to undertake certain actions to produce desired results. The libido, or instinctual drive, causes a man to want to eat, sleep, and reproduce. Deeper, unconscious drives motivate him to achieve other things. Though many reject the Freudian perspective, his work in this area laid a foundation for many theorists who attempted to determine what motivates the human being to do certain things.

The attribution theory holds that some attribute within the individual motivates him to strive toward personal excellence. What is it that prompts the Olympic athlete to run, jump, and suffer for years of enduring work outs with the one hope of some day standing upon the podium and bending forward to have a gold medal draped around his neck? What attribute does this individual possess that others do not? Is there an attribute that does exist that motivates this person to forego immediate for deferred pleasure?

Recent investigations into cognitive constructs, or instincts, wishes, drives, or cravings, explore the individual's striving for excellence. Though this is a rather new perspective, it is again another attempt to explain what motivates individuals to change their behaviors, attitudes, and beliefs and become new people altogether.

Once, handicapped individuals were pigeonholed into believing they needed to accept their physical limitations. A movement developed to change this. First, handicapped people changed their "label." They no longer considered themselves "handicapped" but "physically challenged." Now, each year, Special Olympics are held around the country so physically challenged people can gather and compete against one another just like their sound-bodied counterparts. What motivates the paraplegic to "soup up" his wheel chair, don leather gloves, and spin his wheels along the byways of America just so that one day he can ride at breakneck speed around a quarter-mile track in an attempt to set a world wheel-chair record?

Maslow (1954) maintained that individuals were motivated to meet human needs, the highest of which was to become self-actualized. Before an individual could reach this state, he would need to meet his survival and security needs. He must then fill the need to be wanted or loved and the need to be recognized by others for who and what he is. No person can be self-actualized at all times, and yet, Maslow maintained that all individuals strive to achieve this state.

Is there a personality type or characteristic which possesses more innate motivation than others? What makes a Steven Spielberg or Colonel Sanders achieve the success that others only wish they could? Robbins (1985) maintained that all champions possess seven characteristics which propel them toward realizing their dreams. The first and foremost characteristic is passion. These individuals contain within them a passion to excel. While one made movies that excited eyes and ears, and the other created a famous chicken recipe which pleased the palates of many people world-wide, both, Robbins contended, possessed a passion that made them a cut above the rest of mankind. How did this passion surface in these two men? What about others, the rest of us, who also walk the same face of the earth and want to succeed? With similar passion, can we accomplish the same kinds of extraordinary things these two did?

What comes first, motivation or competence? Are competent individuals more motivated to succeed than others or does some intrinsic, extrinsic, cognitive, attributive, or other innate value or drive prompt an individual to strive for excellence? Is there a personality type which possesses more motivational attributes than another? Is there any connection between personality and motivation, motivation and competence, or is motivation only a concept that we discuss in cognitive terms and still don't have any real notion about what it truly is?

This study attempts to answer some of these questions? Many theories will be reviewed in order to formulate some general principles regarding what motivates human beings. Some motivational techniques will be studied. If we can understand what motivates some people, there is the possibility of replicating these practices with others who are less motivated.

Einstein (1938) wrote that "The formulation of a problem is far more often essential than its solution, which may be merely a matter of mathematical or experimental skill. To raise new questions, new possibilities, to regard old problems from a new angle requires creative imagination and marks the real advance in science."

Motivation is the force. But, what causes it; what feeds it; what accelerates it; what destroys it; are all pertinent questions. No amount of scholarly investigation will produce a definitive answer. However, melding science and the arts together can provide the researcher with a new perspective on what motivates human beings. In this process of reading this text, the reader will understand what motivates others, and most importantly, what motivates him or her to respond to the stimuli of the world and produce goods and services, arts and letters, valued by others of the human species.

2. BEHAVIORAL APPROACHES TO MOTIVATION

In the late nineteenth century psychology merged both philosophy and physiology together in an effort to explain motivational processes in human beings. Three factors caused a revolution in motivational thought. First, there was the explosive growth in theory and methodology of the natural sciences during the previous two centuries. Second, there was the shattering influence of Darwin's theory of evolution. These two influences affected the course of Hull's 1943 formulation (Korman, 1974).

One psychologist profoundly influenced by these three was Watson (1913) who called for psychology to be objective in nature. He called for researchers to study the hard, physical matter of behavior that one could touch, feel, and experiment with in the same way that one could in physiology and physics. Watson believed that in this way psychology could stand beside the other sciences as a legitimate pursuit in the study of man. He declared psychology could operate from the same philosophical framework as these others sciences. The general approach would be to search for the "basic elements" of behavior, physically defined and understood. This basic unit of behavior was called, **conditioned-response**.

This process is known as **Pavlovian Conditioning**. Watson's approach to conditioning is illustrated by the following example.

Stimulus – Response - Action

Watson was able to recondition the child not to fear the rabbit by presenting it in a context where there was no strong fear-inducing stimulus. The child's conditioned fear response was eliminated the same way that it had originally been developed. Watson believed that he had developed a meaningful way of understanding the antecedents to behavioral choice and direction and that he could do it without resorting to what was, for him, the mysticism of conscious experience.

Watson's theories were oversimplified explanations, as he and his followers (Kuo, 1921) thought they would be. The conditioned response (CR) to the conditioned stimulus (CS) is rarely, if ever, the same as the unconditioned response (UR) to the unconditioned stimulus (US). Hence, stimulus substitution cannot account for the change in the direction of behavior, one of the primary concerns of the psychology of motivation. They concluded that something else must be involved. Responses are not infinitely transferable.

Brown (1961) made this same conclusion. He contended that this type of approach would hold that variables such as hunger and thirst, variables which are often called motivational because they arouse and direct behavior, are really just sets of stimuli and act like any other stimuli that become linked to responses through classical conditioning. He described Freud's theory of motivation as follows:

1. Basic instinctual drives serve as determinants of behavioral arousal;

2. Increase in internal stimulation results from cyclic patterns in instinctual drives (id);

3. Nature of instinctual drive that is salient at the time like hunger, thirst, sex, etc., results in motivation to satisfy needs;

4. Societal constraints and values as to appropriate means of instinctual drive reduction (super ego);

5.   Strength of ego in being able to balance demand of id and superego results in need fulfillment;

6.   Contemporary environmental expectancies as to manner in which currently salient instinctual drives may be reduced are developed;

6.   Learned habits as to appropriate means of instinctual drive reduction result in the satisfaction of needs.

7.   Current developmental stages that the person is in (oral, anal, phallic, latency, or genital), reveal preferred habits of drive reduction remaining from earlier stages, frustrations from earlier stages that the individual wishes to overcome;

8.   All this results in the direction of behavior or choice (pp. 112-113).

Freud's theory of motivation was largely untested due to its hypothetical rather than scientific foundation. In avoiding unconscious motivational dynamics, Brown and others moved toward a more scientific and observable treatment of motivation in human beings.

Hull (1943) is remembered today as the author of a sophisticated attempt at constructing a rigorous, locally tight, mathematically oriented theory of motivation. He rejected mental subjective notions, such as the will in favor of physically defined variables in dealing with the phenomena he called motivational processes. His work is described as having involved two major stages, with the first evolving into his 1943 system (Hull, 1943) and the second into his 1952 theory (Hull, 1952).

Hull's theory included the physically oriented behaviorism of Watson and the notions of instinctual behavior stemming from Darwin's theory of evolution. Following Darwin, Hull believed that the problem of arousal of behavior, or why man originally behaved at all, stemmed clearly from evolutionary considerations. Whenever an organism was in a threatening situation, behavior was aroused and engaged in to eliminate the treat. An organism behaved when its survival was threatened, and the direction it took stemmed either from innate behavioral characteristics that had survival value or from learned behaviors that had been associated with survival in the past. Hull believed most forms of behavior could eventually be achieved.

Hull (1943) attempted to provide some clear answers to the "why" of behavior or the reasons certain behaviors were engaged in more than others. He attempted to spell out in precise detail how these mechanisms worked, how they combined, and so on. He proposed that the newborn organism possessed a set of receptors capable of being stimulated by such sources as external stimuli and internal stimuli of the type associated with biological states of a threatening nature. Examples are stomach contractions (hunger), dryness of the mouth (thirst), and tissue injury (pain). These external and internal stimuli give rise to an internal state marked by two major characteristics. The first of these is a general drive state (called **D** by Hull), that acts as a general stimulant to the arousal of behavior in that it stimulates activation of whatever behavior tendencies exist in the organism at the time. The second characteristic is that these biological states have associated sets of physical stimulation unique to each state. Thus, hunger involves stomach contractions, thirst, a dry mouth, and so on, Hull thought, and it is these physical stimuli that determine the direction of behavior. The first type of behavior sequence that might be activated is the unlearned sequence, one innate to the organism possibly bred into him by evolutionary adaptation because of its survival value. The second type of behavior sequence that might be activated is that in which the organism responds to the stimuli using a learned behavior rather than an innately bred mechanism. This learned stimulus-response link Hull called **H**, for habit, and it is on the basis of biological survival value that these stimulus-response links develop, or are learned, or so Hull proposed.

Thus, for Hull, **D**, drive, and **H**, habit, are conceptual, theoretical variables, rather than observable, physical stimuli. They occur and vary as a function of physically defined responses as a function of their values. At least four of the basic instinctual forces of behavior are the desires to reduce (1) hunger, (2) thirst, (3) pain from tissue injury, and (4) sexual stimulation. The 1943 Hullian system postulated a number of determinants and procedures for measuring these determinants. First, **H**, a habit, develops because the responses involved have biological utility in that they have led to the reduction of drive stimuli. The speed and development of **H** is a function of the following variables:

1. The closeness in time of the stimulus-response coupling to the actual stimulus reduction;

2. The number of reinforced trials;

3. The magnitude of reinforcement during training (p. 32)

These procedures determine how **D** and **H** are measured. How do they combine in predicting behavior? Hull, basing his statements on the results of experiments of Perrin (1942) and Williams (1938), suggested that the strength of the impetus to respond is a multiplicative function of habit and drive, assuming the form:

Behavior = f(D) X f(H)

Most forms of complex human behavior cannot be viewed simply as the attempt to satisfy survival needs. These are the forms of motivated behavior that the Hullian tradition tended to report. Human behavior is symbolic, conceptual, and not easily controllable by what seems to be the physical type of external stimulation found in animal experiments.

Hull's proposal was simple but illusory. He proposed that stimuli associated with the primary drive states elicit behaviors similar to those that the primary drive states do. Thus, it was by using the conditioned stimulus-conditioned reinforcers framework developed on the basis of contiguity that Hull proposed to account for complex behavior in his 1943 theory.

Mowrer (1960) proposed a theory of behavior explicitly designed to use much of the Hullian approach and terminology in accounting for complex behavior. His approach dealt with conditioned reinforcers and their implications for controlling behavior. According to Mowrer, various stimuli become associated with various kinds of outcomes and thus assume symbolic significance to the organism. These stimuli assume reinforcing properties and are influences on later behavior. Mowrer distinguished at least four separate cases:

1. Stimuli that become associated with outcomes of behavior that are negative in nature; these become stimuli that are called "fear" stimuli.

2. Stimuli that become associated with outcomes of behavior that are positive.

3. Stimuli that become associated with outcomes of behavior that involve the disappearance of signals that meant the reduction of drives; these become "disappointment" stimuli.

4. Stimuli that become associated with outcomes of behavior that involve the termination of danger stimuli; these become "relief" stimuli.

It was Mowrer's basic prediction that "hope" and "relief" stimuli become positive reinforcers of behavior and can be utilized to build habits since organisms are motivated to achieve them. "Fear" and "Disappointment" are negative outcomes that, Mowrer argued, organisms try to avoid and that will not build up into habits.

Miller (1948) studied how a conditioned response could be predicted. In an experiment with rats, he found that when they were placed in a situation where they would receive shocks while attempting to escape from a maze that they would (a) attempt to escape even before the shock was administered, and (b) learn new habits that would enable escape from the box when earlier learned escapes were unavailable. The implications of this research finding were that fear could be considered a secondary or acquired drive because it acted like a drive even though it was not innate, but was learned, and conditions for its acquisition could be demonstrated experimentally. The fact that the behavior is learned and does not need to have any biological significance attached to it is very crucial. This research was one of the reasons why the adequacy of Hull's theoretical system was eventually challenged by many psychologists.

The significance of anxiety for understanding neurotic behavior had been pointed out by Freud (1933), among others, and psychologists such as Mowrer (1960) spent significant portions of their careers studying the anxiety phenomenon by using experimental techniques inspired by Hullian theory. Miller suggested this in a 1948 article.

> The mechanism of acquired drives allows behavior to be more adaptable in complex variable situations. It also allows behavior to appear more baffling and apparently lawless to any investigator who has not had the opportunity to observe the conditions under which the acquired drive was established. One hypothesis is that neurotic systems, such as compulsions, are habits which are motivated by fear and are reinforced by a reduction in fear (pp. 100-101).

One implication from this successful experimental development of an acquired drive was that it led to a proposed mechanism for integrating within a relatively theoretical framework the diverse multiplicity of human goals. Instead of going through the process of postulating separate motives for such things as money, status, prestige, a new car, a big house, and the like. Brown (1952) suggested:

> The important motivating component of many of the supposed acquired drives for specific goal objects is actually a learned tendency to be discontented or anxious in the absence of these goal objects. On this view, stimulus cues signifying a lack of affection, a lack of prestige, insufficient money, etc. would be said to acquire, through learning, the capacity to arouse an anxiety reaction having drive properties. This learned anxiety would then function to energize whatever behavior is directed toward goal objects by stimuli, and its reduction, following the achievement of these goals, would be powerfully reinforcing (pp. 1-21).

Motivation can be a function of frustration. It is an emotion that causes many people to make life adjustments to meet desired needs. Frustration, according to Brown (1961) and Lawson (1965), is a conflict between two opposing tendencies. One response tendency is the one originally evoked by the situation (presumably some kind of goal response), and the other being some alternative response aroused by the frustrating interfering conditions themselves. This conflict between opposing tendencies leads to whatever could be said to be the unique behavioral consequences of frustration. Because frustration is defined in terms of the relationship between two hypothetical constructs - the opposing response "tendencies" - frustration is a higher order construct. It is defined in terms of first order constructs. One effect is an increase in drive. Frustration adds to the total motivation of the organism, and thus strengthens if the goal directed response is far stronger than any other behavior in the situation. The second effect is to produce unique internal stimuli. These stimuli may be related to other responses not previously present in the situation.

Although there were studies to support Hull's prediction (Wolfe, 1936; Cowles, 1937), the hypothesis always had problems. For example, there was evidence that secondary reinforcers may quickly lose their effect over time if they are not associated often enough with the primary reinforcer (Isaacson, Hutt, and Blum, 1965; Wike, 1969). Other experiments showed secondary reinforcing effects over long periods of time. Zimmerman (1957) predicted that a secondary reinforcer can have long-lasting effects if it has been periodically associated with the primary reinforcer to begin with, rather than a constant association with it. Siegal and Milty (1969) found little experimental support for the proposal that stimuli signal the termination of electric shock take on secondary properties in the manner that Hull and Mowrer predicted.

In his emphasis on Darwinian evolutionary theory as a logic for behavior and on a stimulus-reduction model as a basic explanatory system, Hull (1943) was quite similar to Freud. In other respects he was different. Hull was a physically oriented behaviorist who attempted to deal with motivational processes by postulating physiologically based stimuli of evolutionary significance as leading to the arousal and motivation of behaviors. Once behavior was aroused and drive (**D**) was operative, Hull suggested that direction was due to the linkage of physiologically based stimuli and responses. Despite his objective goals, logical and empirical problems appeared when Hull applied his theories to complex human processes.

Hull's work became what he hoped it would, a stimulation for continued research by opponents and proponents. Fifty years later, his research can still be cited as the acme of what a theory should be: a thought-generating system that proved to be an immeasurable aid in the understanding of what motivates behavior.

There were a number of problems with Hull's 1943 system. While stimuli associated with shock do assume fear or anxiety-arousing properties and do function as drives in the Hullian sense, stimuli associated with hunger and thirst deprivation states do not become conditioned stimuli and do not assume drive characteristics (Cravens and Renner, 1970).

Another set of findings that did not support Hull's work was the evidence that obese individuals do not use biological deprivation cues for how and when they should eat. Their eating behavior seems to be a function of variables of having little or nothing to do with the degree of their physiological deprivation at the time (Nisbett, 1968; Schacter, Goldman, and Gordon, 1968).

As a continuing demonstration of the difficulty of coordinating **D**, as conceptualized by Hull, to biological-need states and the various stimuli conditioned to them, Zajonc's program supported the theoretical assumption that the presence of other people may as a drive state in the Hullian sense. This added to the confusion as to what **D** is (Zajonc, 1965).

There was considerable additional evidence that biologically linked need states as hunger, thirst, pain, and sex area function of many other variables besides physiological determinants. Vernon (1969) pointed out that (a) food preferences are very much culturally determined and some individuals will and do starve rather than eat forbidden foods; (b) sexual behavior is under hormonal influence for organisms low in the evolutionary hierarchy, but such behaviors are very much a function of learning experience for humans and higher animals; (c) there is some basis for biologically linked instinctual maternal behaviors in lower animals but such behavior is culturally determined in humans; and (d) fear and anxiety are very much culturally learned, with great differences between individuals and groups in the degree to which they will admit such reactions and base their behavior on them.

The question is, does the learning of stimulus-response connections (habit) depend on primary and/or conditioned-stimulus (need) reduction?

In a real sense, the logic of Hull's entire approach rested on the answer to this question. He based his system on the principle of the biological utility of behavior and its derivatives. While habits can be learned on the basis of primary or conditioned need reduction, it is not necessary that such reduction occur for learning to take place. The evidence for this statement comes from a variety of research sources, some of which follow:

1.   Non-nutritive saccharin (a substance that passes through the body without providing any food value) can reinforce the learning of an instrumental response (Sheffield and Roby, 1950).

2.   Infant monkeys can obtain satisfaction from ersatz mothers who have not provided milk (Sheffield, Wulf, and Backe, 1951).

3.   Rats can be reinforced by copulating responses without being given the opportunity to ejaculate (Harlow and Zimmerman, 1959).

4.   Habits can be learned when the outcome of the behavior involved is not the reduction of some primary or conditioned need, but rather the opportunity to explore some primary or conditioned need and to explore some "new" stimulus field (Harlow, 1953; Montgomery, 1953; Glanzer, 1953). By a "new" stimulus field is meant one that is different from the one in which the organism is currently behaving and one not previously associated with primary-need reduction.

Blodgett's (1929) famous latent-learning experiments showed quite conclusively that drive reduction, which defines reinforcement in the Hullian sense, seemed to influence engaging in behavior patterns already known, but may not be necessary for learning them. He showed that in three groups of rats learning to run a maze. One of the groups was provided food at the end of the maze whereas the other two were not. At first glance, this seemed to support Hullian theory. However, after closer scrutiny of the data, a different conclusion presented itself. He inferred that both Groups II and III almost immediately attained the level of proficiency of Group I, suggesting that they knew how to run the maze all the time, but that there was no reason to do so. Once they learned that there was food available, there was some reason to show the learned behavior patterns. The latent learning experiments were crucial for at least two reasons. First, by showing that need reduction is not necessary for learning, but that the opportunity for need gratification could generate quick, significant changes in behavior, considerable doubt was cast on the 1943 Hull theory. Second, these results suggested that a complete theory of motivation would have to include some consideration of how changes in the environment affect behavior, and among these effects might be the availability of the types of incentives used by Blodgett. Thus, it was this research that led Hull and his co-workers to develop **K**, a type of environmental incentive, as part of the later 1952 postulates and Spence's 1956 theory.

The theoretically crucial question for Freud, Hull, and other researchers to ask is behavior just a desire to reduce stimulation? Is this where behavior arousal comes from, or is there some other motivating factor present?

Miller and Dollard (1941) suggested a drive is a strong stimulus which impels action. Any stimulus can become a drive if it is made strong enough. The stronger stimulus, the more drive function it possesses.

Their logic eventually led Hull to adopt their argument in 1952. There was considerable evidence to support Hull's, Miller's, Dollard's, and Freud's work. Behavior is sometimes more than just a reduction of stimulation and may lead to less behavior rather than more. The following studies support these notions.

Olds and Milner (1954) found that direct electrical stimulation of certain parts of the brain can reinforce behavior in the same manner as food, thirst, and pain reduction. They found that here was a case where reinforcement can come from more stimulation, rather than less.

Harlow (1953), Montgomery (1953), and Glanzer (1953) all showed that the opportunity to explore and see "newness" and "differences" can be a great incentive to behavior; "newness" and "difference" can be assumed to be increases in stimulation.

Brown and Jacobs (1949) found that increased amounts of drive do not always result in increased physical activity and might actually result in less. As an example, they cited their own research finding that some anxious rats "freeze," rather than increase their motor behavior. This is one of those situations where it is possible to argue that "freezing" is a form of behavior that reduces the drive for the subjects.

Research with different forms of drug addiction and drug-taking behavior indicated both support and difficulties for the Hullian drive concept. On the one hand, the taking of opiates and barbiturates provides support since in these cases the result is some kind of stimulation-reducing process. On the other hand, the taking of hallucinogenic drugs like hashish, marijuana, and LSD, and those termed, analeptic (cocaine and amphetamines), would be considered negative evidence since the outcome is generally increased excitement and stimulation (Cohen, 1965). The sum total of these findings suggest that behavior can clearly be shown to be more than a reduction of stimulation. Under some conditions, organisms may act in order to increase stimulation.

Berlyne's (1960) theoretical hypothesis suggested that the stimulation organisms try to reduce is not environmental but rather in the reticular activating system (RAS) of the brain. Berlyne argued that it is a curvilinear function of physical environmental stimulus complexity, so that RAS arousal is greatest when environmental stimulation is either very great or very small. According to this system, the following behavioral predictions are made as a function of the given physical environmental stimulus condition. The crucial question here is the degree of support for the major innovation of the theory, namely, that low levels environmental stimulation lead to high RAS arousal. While there is some indication that boredom leads to high RAS arousal, the evidence to support this is still scant (deCharms, 1968, p. 101).

The implication of this paradigm is that the previous history of the organism determines its degree of responsiveness to later positive and negative outcomes and how significant these possible or expected outcomes may be in affecting its behavior. The poorer the previous history, the less likely it is that "good" outcomes will be necessary in order to solidify or reinforce approach behavior. The following research studies indicate that the more an organism is punished for its behavior, the less likely it will engage in behavior to achieve rewards and avoid punishments in the future. Conversely, the less it is punished, the more it will be oriented to achieving "good outcomes," such as engaging in behavior to achieve positive outcomes and avoid those that were negative. There is a vast body of research that points to the fact that organisms have not been continuously positively reinforced for engaging in certain behaviors when no reinforcement is available than those who have a history of continuous positive reinforcement.

Baron (1966) found that individuals who have high social reinforcement standards are more likely to perform in a manner designed to achieve high rewards than those who have low social reinforcement standards. Kaufman (1963) and Feather (1965) projected that self-perceived ability on a task based on previous task performance is positively related to later task performance. Korman (1967a, 1967b) hypothesized that individuals of high esteem are more likely to choose occupations where they perceive themselves to have a degree of mobility than those of low self-esteem. In a later study, Korman (1968) found that individuals who are told they are incompetent and cannot achieve specific goals on task, even though they have had no previous experience with the task, will perform worse than those who are told they are competent to achieve the task goals. Zander et al (1969), in studying group behavior, found that if they failed previously set goals, they increase the probability of their failing again. Shaw (1968) maintained that academic underachievers have a more negative self-concept than achievers. Brookover and Thomas (1963-64) found that there is a significant positive relationship between self-concept of ability and grade-point average. Maier's (1949) focused on individuals who had a long series of frustrations. They engaged in behavior that was (a) persistent beyond degree of reward, (b) not alterable by punishments, (c) non-goal oriented, and (d) not affected byconsequences or by the anticipation of the same. Karsh (1962) and Miller (1960) found that human beings often over learned in response to becoming very competent at any task, and this increases as the effectiveness of punishment is meted out resulting in eventually suppressing responses. Miller (1960) supported the notion that human beings adapt to punishment and in so doing decrease its effectiveness to cause change in the individual. Holz and Azrin (1961) found that if a subject is habituated to receiving shock together with positive reinforcement during reward training, punishment during extinction can actually increase resistance to extinction. Masserman's (1943) research indicated that punishment can lead to self-defeating behavior oriented toward no goal. Finally, Miller, Butler, and Martin (1969) concluded that rewarding others has a greater influence on their behavior than punishing them. Spence (1960) and Amsel (1958) theorized that organisms put on a partial-reinforcement schedule learn to link two types of stimuli with approach responses in a given goal-box situation. They learn two habits, not one, under partial reinforcement. The Spence-Amsel attempt to account for what might be termed self-defeating behavior within a physical system received considerable research attention, with some results being supportive (Haggard, 1959; Goodrich, 1959) and others not so (Hill, 1968). These researchers supported the conclusion that individuals will perform in a manner consistent with other reinforcement patterns.

From the previous discussion, it is clear that Hull's 1943 theory had an imposing list of problems that had to be overcome if the approach was to remain a viable one in the study of motivational processes. The decade of the 1950's saw revisions of the general framework by Hull, and his promising student, Kenneth Spence. The dilemma for Hull and Spence was to account for the findings of the latent-learning experiments and others similar to it within the physical system. There was evidence that organisms could and did change their behavior almost immediately when the levels of reward and/or incentive available in the environment changed. This accounted for the fact that behavior was not only determined by previous learning (habit) and current condition (drive), but also by the contemporary characteristics of the environment.

Consider a rat running a maze to get to a "goal box" that has food in it. Once he gets to the food, he begins eating, and the more food, the longer and more vigorously he eats, generally up to the saturation point. Since this eating behavior becomes conditioned by stimulus-generalization processes to the various stimulus characteristics of the "goal box," the rat, when later reintroduced into the "goal box," immediately starts the eating behavior again, even before the food is present. This anticipatory behavior is engaged in prior to actual eating behavior and might be engaged in other parts of the maze prior to actually entering the "goal box." When the rat runs a maze, the physical stimuli affecting him are the stimuli of the maze and his anticipatory goal (or eating) responses at each of the maze prior to the goal (or food) box (Korman, 1974, p. 60).

Spence (1960) described this condition mechanism as **K**, and he felt that **K**, as a general arousing agent acting in the same manner as **D**, should be placed in the same conceptual category.

Behavior = D (drive) **+ K** (conditioned mechanism) **x Habit**

Hull (1952) proposed that **D** and **K** combine multiplicatively, whereas, Spence (1960) proposed that they combine additively, a difference illustrated by the above formula. Hull gave up the simplistic notion that all behavior stemmed from biological-physical sources. He changed his assumption that behavior or drive was aroused by biological-need deprivation by some stimulus conditioned to it. Instead, he eventually supported Miller and Dollard's (1943) assumptions that any strong stimulus can become a drive, the reduction of which is reinforcing. This change in focus presented several advantages. It freed Hull from having to tie all secondary drives back to a biological base and it enabled him to show that, experimentally, learning and performance, and competence, could take place without biological-need reduction.

Five decades after the 1943 model was first presented, there are a number of conclusions that can be waged. First, the tradition is a strong one and remains highly viable as a source for continued resource. Second, environmental as well as biological and sociological factors can and do effect motivational change and Hull and Spence included these factors in their later theories.

As an example of the pervasiveness of the Hullian scheme, Weiss (1968) adopted an approach to delimit the conditions under which attitude change was a function of persuasive communication. He suggested that the likelihood of change as a result of persuasive communication is greater the more we have changed our attitudes in the past. The more anxiety we feel about our current attitudes, and hence the greater the impetus toward change, the more reason we see for attitudinal change.

Zajonc (1965) hypothesized why the presence of others will sometimes facilitate performance and sometimes debilitate it. He postulated that the presence of others is a source of drive, **D**. While other people can be directional influences on behavior in the sense of producing specific cues and reinforcement, Zajonc argued that they are also a source of general arousal, energizing all responses likely to be emitted in the given situation. Zajonc reported a number of studies that supported these predictions (Zajonc and Sales, 1966; Wheeler and Davis, 1967; Cottrell, Rittle, and Wack, 1967; Zajonc, Heingartner, and Herman, 1969). In addition, this particular application was further solidified and related to the general Hullian tradition by the theorizing of Cottrell et al. (1968), Weiss and Miller (1971), and Paulus and Murdock (1971). Evidence suggested by Bolles (1967) that these different sources of drive were not interchangeable in contributing to general arousal and were contrary to Hull's predictions.

Cofer and Appley (1964) created two incentive-like constructs, known as the **sensitization-integration mechanism** (SIM) and the **anticipation-invigoration mechanism** (AIM), as conceptual substitutes for the **D** construct. Berger and Lambert (1968) described these mechanisms as follows:

> The first mechanism (SIM) is posited to explain the invigorating effects on action of selective sensitization to certain stimuli. This effect is probably an innate one, but one that can be modified by learning. For example, under controlled conditions, activity increments which one would expect as a result of deprivation may not occur. These activity increments do occur when the relevant stimuli are introduced, in the sense that the deprived organism responds more vigorously than the non-deprived one. In sex behavior, Beach (1956) suggested hormones are a necessary precondition for arousal of the male, but are not sufficient; usually a receptive female, plus physical or symbolic interaction, are also necessary for copulation to occur. The parallel mechanism, AIM, carries the main weight of the Cofer

and Appley analysis. Here invigoration of behavior is enhanced by learned anticipations. These may take several forms: the incentive cues (K) which "control" anticipation, working through such processes as the r mechanism; the energy released by the states of conflict between two or more anticipations; or the **ee** mechanisms, suggested by Sears (1951). Where anticipation is possible the usual effects of deprivation does not appear to be operative, invigoration may occur through anticipation alone (p. 822).

One major problem with the expectancy system of Hull and Spence was what to predict for low-expectancy people. Do they keep searching for the best alternative and pick that one? Does that mean that before he reaches self-fulfillment drive and habit must be abrogated? Does that mean he is less likely to behave like a high-expectancy person? Many questions remained to be asked by researchers. **K** as a concept did not work because it was logically possible to show that the same processes hypothesized to lead to **K** (behavior increase) would also lead to behavior reduction. In addition to this problem, other logical and empirical problems developed with the Hullian system, suggesting that Hull's goal of achieving an objective, physically oriented, natural-science approach to motivation did not succeed.

3. ACTIVATION AROUSAL THEORY

As a result of the problems developed in the Hullian approach to the study of the motivational process, researchers faced the task of developing new ways of dealing with the psychology of human motivation. This search led to the development of the **Activation Arousal Theory** (AAT).

The overall framework of AAT is summarized in the following statements:

1. Physical stimulation that affects an organism contributes to its physiological and psychological arousal level.

2. The impact of stimulus in terms of its contribution to the arousal level of the organism is a positive function of such variables as its intensity, its meaningfulness, its complexity, the recency of its previous occurrence, the frequency of such occurrences, and the extent to which it provides variation from previous stimulation (Fiske and Maddi, 1961; Walker, 1964).

3. For a given organism at a given time of day, there is a level of arousal that is normal and appropriate for it, and behavior is motivated toward achieving that normal arousal state for that given time of day; having attained that state of normal arousal, its behavior is also motivated toward maintaining that state, in that the organism will engage in behavior designed to increase its arousal level when it is too low and decrease it when it is too high.

4.   Having attained such a state of normal arousal, the organism becomes more sensitive to other aspects of the environment and is more able to deal with them in an efficient manner. If his behavior does not have to be directed toward the achievement of optimal arousal, it can then be directed toward whatever external demands happen to be operating in the environment at the given time. Such increased attention to external environmental demands when an organism is at an optimal activation or arousal level should then lead, all other things being equal, to a U-shaped relationship between arousal level and task performance, since it is when he is in his optimal arousal state that he can pay most attention to task demands (Dember and Earl, 1957; Berlyne, 1960; McClelland, 1955).

AAT postulates that both the arousal and direction of behavior is due to the desire to achieve some kind of "balanced" outcome. It rejects too much stimulation and too little. The current arousal state of the organism determines both the arousal and directive influence on behavior. The degree of arousal and its direction is a function of the degree of deviation from the optimal level. One advantage of this approach is that it does not equate the "desirable" end state of behavior with need or stimulus reduction, a position found seriously deficient in some theories (Eisenberger, 1972). The argument proposes that behavior is oriented toward the achievement of a balanced state of activation. Data supporting the hypothesis were found by Grossman, (1967), and Korman, (1971a).

One of the most significant aspects of AAT is that it conceptually overcomes the weaknesses of the Hull/Freud approach in predicting that behavior ceases once the reduction of the stimulus is achieved. If the organism is in a task situation that is making specific demands for a specific set of behaviors, the prediction of the AAT is that there will be a U-shaped relationship between arousal and performance. The arousal and directedness of behavior is seen as stemming from the task demands of the situation, as well as whatever other specific motivational variables happen to be operating at the time. What is important is that one source of behavior variance is not influencing performance in the optimal arousal situation. Behavior is more controlled by the demands of the external environment and is more effective if it is a setting calling for task performance.

Some interesting research supported the hypothesis by which physical stimuli influence states and related behavior in human beings.

Zlutnick and Altman (1972) found that crowding affected the ability of the organism to control interaction with others or increase the costs of doing so in a physiological and or psychological sense.

Glass and Singer (1972) discovered that the psychological variable of unpredictability, and the anxiety felt because of the lack of control, and it is more important than the physical parameter known as noise intensity in predicting adaptation to noise in task situations. The effect is the same over (a) different procedures for manipulating unpredictability; (b) different levels of physical noise; (c) both male and female subjects; (d) different laboratories.

In a second study, Glass and Singer (1972) found that the concept explained some of the effects of physical stimulation on behavior. They wrote that people who are being exposed to stressful physical stimuli will find it even more intolerable if they are made conscious of the fact that others comparable to themselves are being exposed to stimuli less stressful.

Finkelman and Glass (1970) studied the effect of noise on human performance in terms of its influence on the information-processing capacities of the individual and its tendency to utilize those processes in a manner that increases the capacity of the individual to respond adequately to other stress stimuli. They found that noise adversely affected human performance.

Helson (1964) and Zlutnick and Altman (1972) hypothesized that the effect of any specific type of physical stimulation on an individual is a function of his experience with stimuli of that nature, his expectancy of that situation, and the amount of time he has been in that situation.

One of the advantages of AAT is that theoretically, it may be studied by utilizing physiological and psychological measurements. In each case, the antecedents and the consequences are supported to be the same.

Basically, the findings on the measurement of arousal states can be summarized as follows:

1. There are only moderate correlations between different measures of physiological arousal. This suggests that whatever each of these measures is something separate from the others. The implications are that while there may be a general-arousal state. There are also specific-arousal states (Lacey, 1950).

2. A simple self-report of arousal, either estimated in a general subjective sense (Dermer and Berscheid, 1972) or measured by an adjective checklist (Thayer, 1967) may correlate more highly with physiological measures than the physiological measures correlate with each other. Such simple self-report measures seem to be able to meet fairly demanding construct-validity criteria of the type discussed by Dermer and Berscheid (1972).

AAT tried to account for (a) the fact that people sometimes try to increase as well as reduce stimulation, and (b) the observation that some people differ systematically as to what the desirable types of stimulation are, and (c) that the postulation of biological utility as a rationale for behavior is not assumed. Despite these advantages, AAT presented problems of its own. One of these problems was that the term, arousal, did not describe whether or not we were talking about physiological arousal or a psychological variable. While the two were sometimes related, they did not have to be, since it was comparatively easy to show that the same experimental variables that lead to different results as a function of psychological influences. Finally, the adoption of a curvilinear model posed significant problems for research testing of the approach.

4. COGNITIVE APPROACHES TO MOTIVATION

The contemporary approach in studying human beings is to view the organism as always active, making behavioral-direction choices designed to achieve maximal outcomes. Behavior is viewed as a continuing series of choices designed to obtain the best possible outcomes. The empirical operations for the psychological variables to which causal inferences are attributed have been psychological scale measurements, rather than from mental operations.

While Hull was developing his theoretical system at Yale University, Tolman (1955), at the University of California at Berkeley was creating an alternative approach to motivational phenomena. Tolman viewed motivational behavior as being initiated by various internal and external environmental cues and by disequilibrium situations of various kinds. These cues combined with other characteristics of the organism, such as age, previous training, heredity, and specific physical characteristics of the moment, that result in three major intervening variables. These variables were the major components of Tolman's theory. They were:

(1)   Demands for a specific goal,

(2)   The degree to which the goal is available or exists in the specific environment in which the organism finds itself, and

(3)   His expectancies of achieving the goal in the specific environment in which the organism finds himself.

These three variables determine an organisms direction and persistence of behavior until the goal is reached. He explained his theory in this manner. The demand for a goal could be inferred by the speed with which an organism attacked that specific goal. Goal behaviors are used as operational measures of demand for the goal. The hypothesized causal-agent variable (goal demand) are manipulated by various antecedent conditions that determine goal demand. These manipulations were then studied for their effect on dependent (behavior) variables, which for Tolman were selectivity and persistence of performance of behavior. The **H** (heredity), **A**, (age), and other variables like environmental and physiological stimuli, and previous learning and training effect the expectancy of attaining the goal. Goal availability was factored in to determine if it was currently achievable. The direction of behavior was affected by these preceding factors. If everything proceeded as expected, behavior persistence toward the goal continued and eventually the goal was achieved.

Despite attacks on his theory, Tolman was accurate in his insistence that the persistence and selectivity of performance was both a function of the organism itself and its immediate environment. To understand a specific behavior, it was necessary to study both antecedents of environment and the individual, and not just the latter. It was precisely this mistake that Hull made in 1943 and that he was forced to rectify in 1952 by the introduction of **K**, the incentive variable that reflected the environment the organism was in at that particular time in terms of its particular rewards. For Hull and Spence, environmental expectancy aroused behavior by adding to drive, **(D)**, and directed behavior by providing specific stimuli that activated appropriate directional habits. For Tolman, environmental stimuli may steer and direct behavior by their presence as goals to be achieved in order to satisfy existing demands. Environmental stimuli may also determine expectancies by the degree of their similarity to other environmental conditions whereby specific goals had been sought and achieved in the past (Korman, 1971b, p. 94).

Tolman successfully predicted that behavior would not be expected to occur when the goals and/or incentives to be achieved in the situation by behaving. Rewards affected performance, not learning, a position that Hull and Spence eventually adopted. Given these characteristics of Tolman's theory, he could explain the latent-learning experiment in the following manner, as summarized by Atkinson (1964):

> During the unrewarded trials, the animals develop cognitive expectations of the consequences of turning left or right at each of the various choice points. After several trials in the maze, these forward-pointing expectations constitute a kind of "cognitive map" of the maze that is "refined" during each run...In Tolman's view, a hungry organism is always actively trying to find food. After developing a more refined set of expectations concerning what does lead to what in the maze, the organism comes upon food, a demanded goal-object, in the end-box maze. The next day, as a result of this recent experience added to the cognitive expectations of what leads to what which had been built up without reward in earlier trials, the organism has both a demand for food and an expectation of a food object in the end box when placed in the starting box. The combination of these two determinants accounts for the sudden change in selectivity of performance at each choice point. The organism now selects the "correct" response. (p. 144).

Tolman (1955) viewed the persisting individual-difference characteristics between organisms as important. The individual differences between organisms as determinants of response, holding environmental variation constant, is one of the pervading characteristics of all forms of life. Tolman felt that what an organism did in an experiment was not just a function of how the experimenter varied the environmental conditions. It was a function of who and what the organism was genetically, what his previous learning experiences were, and other individual characteristics. This type of individual, Tolman believed, interacted with the various conditions of the environment and as a result, determined the outcomes, not one or the other alone. Tolman achieved creating the first systematic integration of one theory of logic of contemporary environmental determinants of behavior, and the logic of persisting individual differences in the kinds of goals sought independent of specific environmental variation of the time as joint determinants of behavior.

Even though Tolman's work was significant, he left an incomplete and imperfect system. He recognized this himself and stated so in his writings. First, he never developed any clear statement of how his crucial antecedent variables were interrelated. Second, he never really worked very much on the individual differences in demands and needs that he utilized as constructs in his system. Finally, Tolman never provided an explicit rationale for the arousal of behavior. He never made clear as to when and under what conditions these directional determinants become operative as arousers of behavior.

The historical antecedents to Tolman's work can be traced to Harvard psychologist, Henry Murray (1937). His arguments involved a number of both content and methodological considerations. He believed that the key to the understanding of human personality and motivation would not come from the biological, physiologically based theories of Hull or from insistence on experimental verification of hypotheses in laboratory settings. He felt that much of what was important in human personality would manifest itself in everyday life. Motivational processes could be best observed in naturalistic settings. He argued that individual needs and motives were useful constructs to utilize when studying the psychology of motivational processes.

According to Murray (1937), a need or drive contained both a directional aspect that differentiates it from other needs, and an arousal component that actually precipitates the behavior. The conditions under which the arousal component actually becomes activated in Murray's system were not clear. However, the concept of the end state of behavior being more important than specific behaviors themselves was useful in developing an adequate conceptualization of motivation on the human level for the following reasons:

1. Physical survival depends on achieving certain outcomes, not on what behaviors are used.

2. Certain effects are universally attained by living organisms, but the behaviors that attain them vary greatly.

3. During the life of a single individual, certain effects are regularly attained but the behaviors involved change.

4. When confronted by a novel situation, an organism persists in its efforts to bring about a certain result, but with frustration it is apt to change its mode of attack; hence, the trend is the constant feature and the behavioral mechanisms utilized are the inconstant.

5. There are some effects that can only be attained by entirely novel behaviors.

6. That specific behaviors are secondary is shown by the fact that many biologically necessary effects may be brought about by another person.

7. Complex action is characterized by muscular contractions in widely separate parts of the organism, contractions which manifest synchronous and consecutive coordination. Such organization of movement must be partially determined by a directional process, which is what a need, by definition, is.

8. Presenting a desired end state during a behavior sequence should not stop behavior if external stimuli were the only determinants of behavior. Behavior does end when these sudden presentations of desired end states are made, suggesting that need and the desired end state are the crucial determinants of behavior.

9. When a need is not in a state of readiness, responses to specific stimuli do not occur.

10. When a particular need is active, common objects in the environment may evoke unusual responses, that is, responses that promote the progress of the active need.

11. When a need becomes active, characteristic behavior will usually ensue even in the absence of customary stimuli.

12. It is difficult to interpret without a concept of directional tension experimentally demonstrable phenomena such as the resumption of unpleasant work after interruption; the repetition of once-active trends with different movements; the increase of striving after opposition.

13. There are conscious correlates of desires.

14. Among the commonest subjective experiences is the feeling of conflict between desires.

15. Because of its close connection with happiness and distress, a need is more "important" than a behavior pattern.

16. Experience seems to show that a certain desire may sometimes give rise to a dream or fantasy and at other times, promote direct activity.

17. Introspection and experiment demonstrate that a need may determine the direction of attention and markedly influence the perception and appreciation (interpretation) of external occurrences; to influence sensory and cognitive processes, a need must be some force in the brain region (pp. 112-113).

Murray's arguments raised many questions that more recent research continues to explain. They are:

1. Why do people develop high motives for such goal outcomes as task achievement, or influencing harm on others, or having an orderly world?

2. What do we mean by **pleasure** and why can outcome be pleasurable for one person and another outcome pleasurable for another?

3. Is there one common basis for pleasure as a desired outcome of behavior that can be defined independent of the behaviors designed to achieve it in the same sense used in physiological-need reduction and its derivatives as a basis for motivational behavior?

4. What about achievement, affiliation, order as motivators?

McClelland (1955) answered these questions with the following comprehensive theoretical positions. He summed them up in this manner:

1. A hedonistic explanation for the arousal of behavior is assumed; that is, it is assumed that individuals are motivated to seek pleasant affect and to avoid negative affect.

2. The degree to which a given environmental situation has pleasant or negative affect, and thus will stimulate either approach behavior or avoidance behavior, is defined in a non-circular fashion and stems from discrepancy.

3.   Given this conceptual way of looking at what
        arouses behavior, it follows logically that
        humans are motivated to achieve end states that
        involve a moderate discrepancy from previous
        adaptation levels to avoid end states that involve
        extreme discrepancies from previous adaptation
        levels (p. 215).

Considering its non-circular aspects and its considerations of the arousal problem, McClelland's theory was a major conceptual step in the development of an adequate expectancy-value theory of motivation. The actual end goal of behavior is defined differently and independently of the sources of the behavioral arousal. The end goals are the attainment of moderate discrepancies from the previous stimulus adaptation level and the avoidance of extreme discrepancies.

5. CONSISTENCY THEORY OF MOTIVATION

The notion that motivational processes may be described as being homeostatic in nature has a long tradition and can be found in the writings of a number of different fields beside psychology. Summer (1906) wrote that a "strain toward consistency" in cultural norms and folkways can be a thesis describing man's motivation. Cannon (1939) originally coined the term, **homeostasis**, meaning the steady state the physiological processes were aimed at achieving. Cofer and Appley (1964) cited a number of studies to support this theory. Stagner (1951) noted that perceptual tendencies were a prime example of the human organism's desire to maintain a steady state. Korman (1971b) found that task and work behavior can be and often are kept at a steady level despite considerable variation in such environmental stimuli as noise and music. Festinger (1941) found that goal setting was positively influenced by task success thus supporting the homeostatic model.

Some criticisms of the consistency theory abounded. Young (1949) proposed that the consistency theory cannot handle the observed data that organisms will sometimes seek non-nutritive substances resulting in an imbalance in the homeostatic state of the being. Another criticism was that the consistency theory could not account for creativity, suicide, or self-sacrificing behavior (Maddi, 1968). In terms of accounting for suicide and/or self-defeating behavior, there was nothing in the consistency theory that necessarily precluded predicting such behavior when the primary units under analysis were psychological in nature, rather than physiological. It was this concentration on psychological imbalance that marked the contemporary work in consistency motivation.

Imbalances make the world more anxiety prone provoking frustration in humans. Since not knowing how others will react and behave makes it difficult to satisfy human desires and motives adequately, humans often behave and reward themselves in a consistent fashion so that they may know and understand the world better, and thus satisfy their needs (Brehm and Cohen, 1962; Baron, 1968). Humans engage in consistent behavior because it makes them more credible and understandable in the eyes of others. Having such status enables them to influence others in order to achieve particular goals (Tedeschi, Schlenker, and Bonoma, 1971). There was evidence to support the hypothesis that imbalance may be considered as a secondary source of drive in a Hullian sense. However, evidence both for and against this proposition existed (Pallak and Pittman, 1972; Seudfeld and Epstein, 1971).

There was considerable evidence to support the basic assumption that psychological imbalance was under some conditions a sufficient condition for the arousal and direction of behavior aimed at reducing that imbalance. Jordan (1953) tested and supported the hypothesis that hypothetical imbalanced situations would be rated as more unpleasant than hypothetical balanced situations (Whitney, 1971). Zajonc and Burnstein (1965) found that triads about relevant issues were balanced and learned more rapidly than those that were imbalanced. For irrelevant issues, balance did not have an influence on learning. People who interact frequently were more apt to like one another according to Homans (1950) and Festinger, Schacter, and Back (1950). Knowledge that one had been assigned somebody else as a partner increased the attractiveness of the other person even before personal contact with the individual was made (Darley and Berscheid, 1967). Using the galvanic response (GSR) as a measure of emotionality in balanced and unbalanced situations, Burdick and Byrnes (1958) found that (a) GSR differed depending on whether the subjects agreed or disagreed with a well-liked experimenter, and (b) subjects who liked an experimenter tended to change their opinions toward greater agreement with him, while those who disliked him tended to change their opinions toward greater disagreement.

Congruity, as developed by Osgood and Tannenbaum (1955) was in its basic orientation a special case of balance theory as developed by Heider, the identity was in some respects a misleading one. The reason it was misleading was that congruity theory, as opposed to consistency theory, was far more sophisticated in terms of its measurement aspects and its preciseness of its predictions. Its advance in measurement were limited. The cost of congruity theory was more limited in scope than most theories. First, it dealt with the problem of predicting the direction of attitude change as a function of the nature and characteristics of attitude-change messages. Second, it dealt with the prediction of how complex stimuli will be evaluated as a function of the simple stimuli out of which they are constructed (Tannenbaum, 1968). There were two basic assumptions of Osgood and Tannenbaum's congruity theory:

1. Evaluative judgements tend toward maximal simplicity. Since "black or white," "all or nothing," or "you're with us or against us" evaluative judgments are easier to make than more refined, differentiated ones, there is continuing pressure within the cognitive structure toward judgements of this nature, and toward the polarization of one's opinions.

2.   Since seeing two things as being identical is less complex than seeing them as being finely discriminated from one another, related concepts will tend to be brought together within one's cognitive structure and related to one another in a similar manner (p. 162).

Given these basic assumptions, the principle of congruity purported that attitude change will always occur in the direction of increased congruity with the prevailing frame of reference. It was the basic prediction of congruity theory that when sources of statements and objects of statements were linked by an assertion in an incongruous fashion, there will be a tendency to change attitudes toward both the source and the object in the direction of increased congruency. The change will take place dependent upon whether or not the assertion is positive or negative in terms of how it links the person making the assertion and the object of the assertion. It also depends on how the person feels about the source and object and the strength of these feelings. The degree of change will also depend on how discrepant these attitudes are to begin with.

Along with consistency theory, congruity theory generated a great amount of research, a fact that was surprising considering its general sophistication and the preciseness of its predictions. While it did possess weaknesses by not providing a means for assessing the strength of assertions or for the fact that incongruity reduction may take place in ways not specified by the theory, these weaknesses were relatively common to all consistency theories. While the others did not have the strengths of the congruity approach, it was somewhat puzzling that the amount of research generated was small compared to other consistency theories.

No discussion of consistency motivation would be complete without mention of cognitive dissonance, a theory generated a significant degree of research and controversy. The logic of dissonance theory was originally developed by Festinger (1957). It was quite simple at first glance. The basic postulates of the theory were:

1. Man has cognitions about the world and about himself (cognitions are bits of knowledge, attitudes, and perceptions).

2. These cognitions may have three forms of relationship with one another within the individual's cognitive apparatus.

3. One relationship is that any two cognitions may be consonant with one another. By consonant, Festinger meant that one cognition follows from the other. For example, when a person who enjoys watching a baseball game goes to one.

4. A second type of relationship between any two cognitions is that they may be irrelevant to one another. For example, a person who enjoys watching baseball games decides to have ham and eggs for supper.

5. A third type of relationship between any two cognitions may be that they are dissonant with one another in that considering the two cognitions alone, the observe of one would follow from the other. For example, a dissonant relationship would be that the person who likes watching baseball games goes to the opera even though there is a game being played that he could attend (Korman, 1974, p. 167).

According to Festinger, dissonance was a negative motivational state that one wished to reduce when it occurred. The occurrence of dissonance was postulated to serve as an antecedent to condition leading to the arousal of behavior. Direction was a function of choosing those behavioral alternatives that will reduce the dissonance. It could be avoided through such processes as selective information seeking and the like. Festinger postulated that the total amount of dissonance a person felt was a function of the total number of units that were in a dissonant relationship with one another, weighted by the importance of the cognitive elements involved. The basic prediction was that the greater the amount of dissonance, the more likely behavior will be undertaken in order to reduce the dissonance. Thus, motivation to change was directly related to the dissonance a human being felt.

One of the most intriguing derivations made by dissonance theory was its predictions concerning the problem of partial reinforcement. The problem was that clear behavioral regarding organisms reinforced the learning on a partial-reinforcement schedule and would persist in the learned behavior longer after reinforcement was totally withdrawn. In a series of experiments, Festinger and Lawrence (1962) proposed that the partial-reinforcement effect was nothing but a manifestation of the forced compliance predictions.

The question the motivational researcher must ask is, if consistency is such an important motivational variable, why are there inconsistencies in human cognition? Bem (1970) suggested that consistency may not be important for some people. Those who are not intellectually oriented and who do not care particularly about the degree to which they present a logical, coherent, consistent picture of the world, express the limitations that are the essence of the consistency theory. Consistency motivation seemed to be an important influence on behavior.

There are three reasons consistency theory remained a popular approach in interpreting motivational theory for a period of time. First, it generated frequently supported, subtle, non-obvious predictions. Second, consistency theory had great appeal to those psychologists who want to investigate questions of a more human, as opposed to animal, bent, but who still wanted to be relatively rigorous and experimentally oriented in their thinking and research. Finally, what was most significant, the consistency approach remained viable for the same reasons as the other theories presented above. If the consistency approach was to remain viable, attention would have to be paid to such questions as (a) the measured degree of inconsistency in a person at a give time, (b) individual differences in the type of inconsistency reduction preferred, and (c) the conditions under which it will not (i.e., the inconsistency is tolerated as a "fact of life").

6. ACHIEVEMENT MOTIVATION

What is it that causes some people to be highly motivated to perform well when assigned a task? What is it about them that makes them willing to undertake the behaviors necessary designed to achieve a task-success experience and others are not? Questions such as these are at the core of the study of achievement motivational processes. Psychologists interested in mental health and life satisfaction find that for individual human beings, the act of achieving is highly important for satisfaction with the self (Korman, 1971b). Knowing what conditions determine the arousal and direction of behaviors for these achievement-seeking individuals, permits psychologists and educators to plan for a therapeutic and educational interventions and increase the likelihood of life achievement (Aronson and Carlsmith, 1962).

Cognitive dissonance research provided one bit of evidence for the fruitfulness of the consistency rationale in understanding some of the conditions that lead to achievement motivation. Some general research findings supported this position. Adams and Rosenbaum (1962) found that when a person is paid by piecework, his productivity will be greater when he perceives his piecework rate is deserved than when he feels it is not deserved. Adams and Jacobsen (1964) studied subjects who, not believing that they had the qualifications to earn a given piecework rate, produced better quality and less quantity work than those individuals who perceived they had the qualifications to earn a given piecework rate. Denmark and Guttentag (1967) discovered that women with self-esteem who want to go to college are more likely to engage in behaviors designed to achieve that goal than women who want to go to college who have low self-esteem. Andrews (1967) showed that subjects who perceive that they are getting a higher piecework rate than they deserve, based upon previous experience, decrease their performance, while individuals getting less than they perceive they deserve increase their performance. Aronson, Carlsmith, and Darley (1963) found that people who expect that they will have to do something unpleasant on the basis of previous experience choose to perform the unpleasant task, even when they could have chosen a more pleasant one. Walster, Aronson, and Brown (1966) and Rosekraus (1967) studied people who anticipated an unpleasant experience voluntarily and found that they endured more shock than those anticipating a pleasant or unspecified experience.

In western civilizations, it is common to hear the argument that people are motivated to achieve as a function of the value the human being expects to obtain by this behavior. This is nothing more or less than the application of the expectancy-value framework. The acceptance of the expectancy-value approach to achievement motivation is so embedded within human beings that it provides the theoretical basis upon which most of the administrative practices commonly found in formal organizations are traditionally founded. In organizations the controlling influence, usually the administration, decides that there are certain gratifications that most people want from school and/or their jobs which the administration controls. The administration controls and increases achievement by making the attainment of these rewards contingent upon effective performance. The promise of such value attainment will result in increased performance. The possible outcomes will serve as incentives for better performance provided the individual involved believes the rewards actually are attainable on the basis of his efforts. If he believes that such rewards are not contingent on his performance, he will not react to them as incentives.

Lawler and Porter (1967) studied this type of expectancy-value approach in work achievement. Their hypothesis was that the amount of effort a person expended on his job (as judged by his superior or peers) was related to the extent to which he perceived he could achieve desired outcomes by engaging in such effort. A number of studies showed similar results (Georgopoulos, Mahone, and Jones, 1957; Hackman and Porter, 1968; Gailbreath and Cummings, 1967; Goodman, Rose, and Furcon, 1970). It was generally concluded that the adequacy of this type of expectancy-value theory was useful in accounting for performance variation in achievement situations.

The Porter-Lawler approach was only one way in which the expectancy x value framework was applied to the study of achievement-oriented behavior. McClelland (1955) contributed another theoretical basis by arguing that achievement motivation develops in some people more than in others because for some people achievement outcomes have positive effect, that is, these outcomes are only of moderate discrepancy from what has been previously experienced. He outlined his basic rationale as follows:

1.   Individuals differ in the degree to which they find achievement a satisfying experience.

2.   Individuals with a high need for achievement tend to prefer the following situations and will work harder in them than individuals of low achievement:

a. Situations of moderate risk - the rationale for this is that feelings of achievement will probably not occur in cases of great risk.

b. Situations in which knowledge of results is provided - the rationale for this is that a person with a high degree of achievement motivation will want to know whether he has achieved or not.

c. Situations in which the individual responsibility is provided - the rationale here is that a person oriented toward achievement will want to make sure that he, and not somebody else, gets the credit for it.

3. Since the business entrepreneurial role has the characteristics outlined in 2a, b, and c, the individuals of high need for achievement will be attracted to the entrepreneurial role as a lifetime occupation (p. 193).

According to McClelland's original frame-work, achievement should not have the parameters of moderate risk-taking, quick feedback, and individual responsibility. Yet such relationships do occur (Cummings, 1967). This suggests that what is actually being measured is a general performance capability in real-life situations and not performance variation as a function of different kinds of task and risk situations. Support for the moderate risk-taking notion, a key aspect of the theory, was highly controversial (Kogan and Wallach, 1967). The reason for this was that in experimental studies in which this aspect had been supported, the level of difficulty was defined by the experimenter, the one who has decided what should be labeled a hard, moderate, or easy task (Atkinson and Litwin, 1960).

In the area of achievement motivation itself as a specific content question, it was proposed that several kinds of cognitive activities can take place as a result of a behavior that has led to achievement (Weiner et al., 1972). These cognitive activities and their hypothesized outcomes were described as follows:

Expectancy

Stimulus > Cognitive Achievement >Behavior>Affect

Weiner's (1972) argument that high and low need achievement individuals differed significantly. The high achievement person was more likely to attribute success to his own efforts. There was some evidence that different motivational processes may be involved in achieving as an individual and achieving within a group. A strong ego was viewed to be of considerable value for achievement as an individual (Korman, 1971b; McClelland, 1961). On the other hand, it was detrimental when trying to achieve within a group where sublimination of the self may be necessary (Collins and Guetzkow, 1962).

Future research question regarding achievement motivation that need to be asked are the two sets of findings reconcilable and under what conditions?

7. MOTIVATION TOWARD AGGRESSION

Regarding other specific forms of motivated behavior that are frequently studied because of their significance to societal and personal functioning, the motivation to hurt others, or the motivation toward aggression is of significant interest to researchers.

Dollard et al. (1939) published **Frustration and Aggression**, a text whose main thesis clearly and unequivocally maintained that: "Aggression is always a consequence of frustration," and "occurrence of aggressive behavior always presupposes the existence of frustration and, contrariwise, the existence of frustration always leads to some form of aggression." Therefore, a one-to-one relationship between "frustration" is postulated. The authors then carefully defined as a condition which exists when a goal response suffers interference (p. 11)." Whenever any type of aggressive act occurs, such an act, according to the hypothesis, is always due to some frustration or interference with a goal response the organism suffered, and conversely, whenever an organism suffers any kind of thwarting or frustration, it will aggress (Kaufman, 1970, pp. 24-25).

As the years progressed, the weakness of the frustration-aggression hypothesis started to become apparent. It was quickly pointed out that often goal-directed responses were interfered with, yet aggression did not take place. Considerable aggression did often take place despite frustration of a relatively minor nature (e.g., the Nazi persecution of the Jews). These findings and other questions relating to the theory were eventually used by Berkowitz (1962) as the basis for a revised formulation of the hypothesis.

Berkowitz (1962) maintained that the frustration-aggression hypothesis contained three basic tenets:

1.   The greater the frustration, the greater the instinct to aggression.

2.   There is the prediction that the stronger the behavioral motive being frustrated, the greater the impulse to aggression.

3.   The greater the number of frustrations, the greater the aggressive response (p. 32).

Berkowitz concluded that only the first two hypotheses could be supported. The data on the third suggested not a linear relationship as proposed but, a curvilinear one, in that aggression as a response to frustration will increase with the number of frustrations up to a point. It will then decrease. He believed that expectancies seemed to be the major answer. As the number of frustrations increased, a person comes to expect them. When a frustration does occur, the reaction is not as negative, or so the data seemed to indicate. Berkowitz wrote:

> In general, expected frustrations produce less intense emotional reactions than do unanticipated frustrations. Two reasons are suggested: (1) through anticipating interference with his activity, the individual may alter his actions, or even his goals, so that he actually experiences less frustration; (2) expected frustrations may be judged as less severe (pp. 72).

Other research evidence revealed the following conclusions that were integrated into Berkowitz's hypothesis:

1.   Aggressive behavior as a response to frustration is inhibited when punishment for such behavior is expected.

2.   Hostile behavior is inhibited the greater the degree of punishment that is expected.

3.   High-status people are usually less likely to be aggressed against than low-status individuals. This supports the general principle because high-status people are more likely to control the likelihood of obtaining other desired goals .

4.   The groups and individuals who are usually chosen as scapegoats and as targets of aggressive behavior are usually weaker individuals who have not the strength to fight back at the aggression; hence, this makes the aggression more likely to be successful (Davies, 1962).

5.   The likelihood of revolution as a function of frustration is more apt to take place after a period of rising expectations (Wallace, 1971).

Another major body of research literature falls under the heading of **modeling**, or watching the effects of the behaviors of others on one's own behavior. Bandura and Walters (1963) focused on the conditions under which models and modeling might be used as a mechanism for changing the behavior of aggressive people. They found that the cessation of some punishment is more likely to be repeated by the observer than if the behavior is punished. Bandura, Ross, and Ross (1963) made the rather simple assumption that people learn about attainable values by observation. Feshbach and Singer (1971) found that boys who watched aggressive behavior on television were less likely to be aggressive than those who did not watch television violence. This was directly opposite from the modeling studies and from the general expectancy-value framework. Recent research into the relationship of television violence on aggression is still inconclusive.

Walsters and Berscheid (1972) proposed the inequity theory to explain aggressive behavior. They maintained that inequity is a negative tension state that people want to reduce. They cited the following propositions:

1.   Under some conditions, a person will feel inequity because he receives outcomes higher than he perceives he deserves. Such tension may result because this would violate the societal norms of equity that underlie the basic equity assumption and because of a fear of retaliation for this equity violation.

2.   A person may reduce his feelings of inequity, under certain conditions, by (a) derogating the other person in terms of the value of the other person's inputs into the system, thus reducing the necessity for higher outputs; (b) minimizing the other person's inputs, thus increasing relative output; and (c) denying the fact of one's responsibilities for the lack of value (or outputs) that the other person receives (p. 216).

The rapidity of change and the resultant aggressive behavior are the current focus of many researchers. Among the highly stable phenomena that can be counted on in a rapidly changing world is the level of unplanned and random violence is increasing. Any casual observer of today's events is assaulted by the crime on the streets, the senseless murders and beatings of innocent people, and other similar aggressive events. The question researchers are asking is what is causing it? Zimbardo (1969) outlined a **Model of Deindividuation and Aggression**. He wrote:

Deindividuation is a complex, hypothesized process in which a series of antecedent social conditions lead to changes in perception of self and others, and thereby to a lowered threshold of normally restrained behavior. Under appropriate conditions what results is the "release of behavior in violation of established norms of appropriateness." Such conditions permit overt expression of antisocial behavior, characterized as selfish, greedy, power-seeking, hostile, lustful, and destructive. However, they also allow a range of "positive" behaviors which we normally do not express overtly, such as intense feelings of happiness or sorrow, and open love for others. Thus, emotions and impulses usually under cognitive control are more likely to be expressed when the input conditions minimize self-observation and evaluation as well as concerns over evaluation by others. We may speak loosely of: conditions of deindividuation (conditions stimulating it), the feelings or state of deindividuation (the experiential aspect of the input variables together with the inferred subjective changes), and deindividuated behaviors (characterized by several specific output behaviors). Deindividuation refers to the entire process and only then becomes a unique psychological construct (p. 254).

This is one attempt by a psychologist to account for the increasing violence in America today. More evidence is needed as Zimbardo suggested himself. What is important about his work is that he attempted to explore why deindividuation results in greater aggression. His hypothesis was basically that violence was an instinctual general drive, and he argued that humans desire to avoid controls and dowhat nature tells them to do. Increasing change leads to increasing frustration as such increasing frustration leads to an increased propensity for aggression. It is more likely to occur because external controls inhibiting the aggression (possible punishment) have decreased in salience due to the rapid change.

Deindividuation theory received minimal focus by researchers. No significant correlations have been proven to adopt it as a definitive answer to the exponential increase of street violence in America. Aggression motivation needs to be studied further not only to validate what causes it, but more importantly, how to curtail it given its detrimental effect on individuals, families, communities, and the civilization it currently is affecting with dire results.

8. MOTIVATIONAL THEORY OF CHANGE

The motivation to accept change falls somewhere between the behaviorists' approaches and the aggression theories. Korman (1974) argued that in American society people must do at least three things if they are to live their lives effectively. First, they must achieve on tasks, whatever those tasks might be. Second, people must be able to keep interpersonal conflict and aggression toward others under sufficient control so that such behavior will not become debilitating and consume so much time and effort that personal goals cannot be achieved. Third, people must possess the capacity to be creative and change if the environment calls for it. This last condition is important in today's dynamic society because of the exponential rates of change people face.

Korman (1974) maintained that an integrated theory of motivational processes of change contain these three components:

1. Motivational processes are a function of the drive to be consistent with belief systems about the nature of the self, others, and the world.

2. Belief systems leading to differing levels of achievement, creativity, and aggression are a function of and develop in the same environments.

3. Changing environments in certain directions specified by the theoretical model will result in changes in achievement, creativity, and aggression (p. 226).

Korman believed humans are motivated first, to achieve outcomes that are consistent with their evaluative beliefs about themselves, and their evaluative beliefs about others, and the degree to which they believe that there is one set of values to guide behavior in this world. Second, humans learn about themselves, others, and the world as a function of the actual and symbolically stated opinions of others. Thus, holding other learning experiences about the self and others constant, the more the individual human being interacts with a world that encourages a certain system of beliefs about the self, others, and the world, the more these beliefs become part of the individual. The motivation to change becomes a function of three different facets of a human being's life experience (Korman, 1974, p. 228). The more these three are integrated together in an effective manner, the more successful the individual will be in living his or her life.

Festinger (1954) supported this position by maintaining that humans are motivated to learn about self and others and establish a socially real world. He wrote that in a world of social behavior, since there is no physical reality, the only way for a person to establish a system of evaluative beliefs about the self and others and the variability of the world is to interact with others, both overtly and symbolically. He made the following predictions:

1.   People of high self-perceived competence and positive self-image should be more likely to achieve on task performance than those who have low self-perceived competence, low success expectancy and low self-image concerning the task or job at hand. Since such differential task achievement would be consistent with self-cognitions, people view task performance as valuable.

2. People who have beliefs that there is one set of rules to guide behavior in this world and that there is one way of looking at the world are more likely to be opposed to creative change, change in general, and to those people or things that are different or constitute a change from themselves, since such change would be inconsistent with their belief systems.

3. People who have beliefs that people, in general, are not desirable, cannot be trusted, and must be controlled by threats and punishments are more likely to develop aggressiveness toward others and are more likely to engage in generally hostile interpersonal behavior, since such types of behavior would be consistent with their belief systems about people (p. 290).

There is considerable research to support the findings of Korman and Festinger. Erlich and Lee (1969) and Torcivia and Rokeach (1968) found that dogmatism in people is negatively correlated with the ability to learn new beliefs. Restle, Andrews, and Rokeach (1964) proposed that highly dogmatic individuals are more likely to learn problems involving the simple following of authority, while low dogmatists are more likely to do well on problems involving the learning of new principles. Druckman (1967) found in people a resistance to compromise with the other side during collective bargaining (simulated) and the tendency to use unilateral planning (as opposed to bilateral discussion) is positively correlated with dogmatism scores. Eckhardt and Newcombe (1969) discovered that dogmatism loads heavily on the same factor with authoritarianism and a belief in militarism and an aggressive foreign policy. Fillenbaum and Jackman (1961) found that dogmatism is negatively related to the likelihood of rejecting standard operating procedures and developing new procedures into a working system. Vacchiano et al (1969) showed that dogmatism is negatively related to looking for new approaches in music, art, and films. In a separate study, the same team found that dogmatism is negatively related to acceptance of liturgical change among Catholics and acceptance of technological change in the factory. Lastly, Berkowitz (1962), in studying Europe before the second world war, found that dogmatism is positively correlated with dislike of dissimilar religions. It is clear that dogmatism adversely affects the motivation to change when new and dynamic situations are presented to the individual.

Environment often affects how individuals adapt. The following studies showed that environment does have a significant effect on how effectively the individual accepts change in his/her life. Domino (1969) found that mothers of creative high-school males valued autonomy and independence, preferred change and lack of structure, and exhibited great self assurance. The mothers of a control group scored lower on all these variables. Adams (1968) found that the creation of an experimental atmosphere with decreased evaluation by others and perception of control and evaluation by others resulted in higher scores on tests of creative thinking. Buetzkow (1965) discovered that innovativeness in organizations is negatively related to hierarchical centralization of authority and positively related to lack of programming and rule orientation. Regarding change in an environment, Coch and French (1948) studied how, in a decreasing hierarchy with external controls and task specialization, a "change" program increased receptivity to the goals of the "change." Strain, Unikel, and Adams (1969) found that middle-class subjects were more likely to engage in alternative behavior than those from lower-class backgrounds. Their contention was that middle class environments were discovered to be generally less hierarchical than the lower class. Korman (1970) showed that individuals in college environments where hierarchical control, programming, and specialization have been de-emphasized are more likely to accept continuing changes in the university and its functioning. Korman (1963) and Sutton and Porter (1968) found that individuals in specialized roles and occupations were more likely not to sympathize with people different from themselves and were less likely to communicate with such different individuals on an informal basis. Related to creativity, Maier and Hoffman (1961) showed that individuals who were employed in hierarchical organizations do more poorly on creative tasks than those who have not been employed by such organizations. Hoffman, Harburg, and Maier (1962) discovered the correlation between creativity and an individual's position related to his or her supervisor. In a less hierarchical system, creativity was fostered in individuals who were not subjected to the control of their supervisors. In studying group behavior, Ziller, Behringer, and Goldstein (1962) discovered that groups which experience changes in membership were more creative than those that were stable. Steiner (1965) showed that organizations that hire unusual, different types of people, were more likely to be creative organizations. Watson (1960) and Getzels and Jackson (1962) found that creative children come from homes (a) marked by a lack of parental dominance and structures, and (b) where individual divergence was permitted and risk accepted. From these studies, environment can be seen to be a major factor in affecting how an individual develops within the context of his or her society.

9. MASLOW'S THEORY OF SELF-ACTUALIZATION

Self-actualization theory was based upon the work of the existential philosophers. It argued that man possesses the capability for a meaningful, viable, potential-filling existence, and that he has the properties and the nature to implement a meaningful existence, but that he has been prevented from engaging and behaving in this meaningful, self-actualizing manner by the conditions and environments in which he lives. He is forced to behave in some suboptimal manner in which he is not able to fulfill himself (or self-actualize) because of the nature of the environmental forces that surround him. Maslow (1954, 1968) that was the founder of the self-actualization movement in America.

It began when Maslow (1970) revised his original text, Motivation and Personality because he believed "the irritating fact is that this veritable revolution (a new image of man, of society, of nature, of science, of ultimate values, of philosophy, etc.) is still almost completely overlooked by much of the intellectual community, especially that portion of it that controls the channels of communication to the educated public and to youth. For this reason, I have taken to calling it the Unnoticed Revolution (p. 10).

Many professional community members, he observed, maintain a negative outlook on the future. They:

1. Exhibit a profound despair and cynicism which emanates from a belief that there is corrosive malice and cruelty present in the world and there is not much that can be done about it.

2. Doubt the "realness of honesty, of kindness, of generosity, of affection, and go beyond a reasonable skepticism or a withholding of

judgment into an active hostility when confronted by people whom they sneer at as fools, innocents, do-gooders, or Pollyannas (Maslow, 1970, p. 2).

Given such a world view, Maslow (1970) believed the only solution to end the despair was to accept a holistic concept of reality. His hypothesis was that the holistic way of thinking and seeing seemed to come quite naturally to healthier, self-actualizing people, and seemed to be extraordinarily difficult for less evolved, less mature, less healthy people. Maslow used this approach in clinical, social, and experimental ways. He found that it fit well with the personal experience of most people. A structured theory like his made it possible for people to make better sense of their personal lives. He admitted his theories lacked experimental verification and support, but in time he believed, his theories would be validated by research.

McGregor (1960) applied this holistic theory of motivation to the industrial situation and found that it was useful in ordering his data and observations. From the industrial rather than the laboratory setting, empirical support developed for Maslow's hierarchy of needs theories.

According to Maslow (1970) human life can never be fully understood unless its highest aspirations are considered. Growth, striving toward good health, the quest for identity and autonomy, self-actualizing which results in a yearning for excellence in whatever the individual does, need to be accepted as the most universal human tendencies (p. 3). He believed:

> ...that if we become fully aware of these human traits, if we can give up the dream of permanent and uninterrupted happiness, if we can accept the fact that

we will be only transiently ecstatic and then inevitably discontented and grumbling for more, that then we may be able to teach the general population what self-actualizing people do automatically, i.e., to be able to count their blessings, to be grateful for them, and to avoid the traps of making either/or choices (p. 17).

In order for the individual to overcome the lows and highs in life, he will need to undertake the delicate task of trying to uncover his temperament or personality type so that he can grow unhampered in his own individual style. Though Maslow (1970) believed that self-actualizing subjects transcended nationalities, class, and caste, he accepted, a priori, that affluence and social dignity make them more probable.

A priori plans for a child, ambitions for it, prepared roles, even hopes that it will become this or that, all these are non-Taoistic according to Maslow (1954). They represent demands upon the child that it become what the parent has already decided it should become. Such a baby is born into an invisible straitjacket. In order to overcome this dilemma, the individual needs to seek his own identity, his own needs, and his own level of self-actualization. Maslow assumed:

The actualization of a person's real potentialities is conditioned upon the presence of basic-need satisfying parents and other people, upon all factors now called "ecological," upon the "health" of the culture, or the lack of it, upon the world situation, etc. Growth toward self-actualization and full human-ness is made possible by a complex hierarchy of "good preconditions." These physical, chemical, biological, interpersonal, cultural conditions matter for the individual finally to extent that they do or do not supply him with the basic human necessities and "rights" which permit him to become strong enough, and person enough, to take over his own fate (p. 24).

In the search for what motivates the individual, methods, techniques, and logic often get in the way. This does not minimize the need for some orderly procedures in attempting to understand what is clearly in the affective domain of the human being. However, many scholars write big monographs on little subjects. Some call this effort "original research." What matters to them most is that they find facts that were not known before, not that the facts are worth knowing. Their justification for their work is that some other specialist might sooner or later make use of them. The specialists, like mound builders, write for one another, for mysterious ends (Van Doren, 1936). The need to seek new explanations for old behaviors and beliefs is necessary for the advancement of the human body of knowledge. Tradition in science and sociology can be a dangerous blessing. Loyalty is an unqualified peril.

Anshen (1934) believed humans "tend to do things that we know how to do, instead of trying to do things that we ought to do (p. 446). Motivation is a part of this "ought" in human life. Humans take few risks because they are unwilling to fail and thereby diminish their own self-esteem. MacLeish (1954) maintained "It is the questions that we do not know" that prompt research regarding motivation and change. Hence, we must continue to ask, what motivates people?

Maslow's (1954) theory incorporated sixteen propositions that he believed must be considered when making any sound explanation of what motivates human beings.

1.   The Individual as an Integrated Whole

The first proposition stated that "the individual is an integrated, organized whole." In Maslow's framework, this means many specific things. The whole individual is motivated rather than just part of him. There is no such thing as just the need of the stomach, or mouth, or a genital need. There is only the need of the individual. Bert Nemcik wants food, not just Bert Nemcik's stomach. Satisfaction comes to the whole individual and not just to part of him. Food satisfies Bert Nemcik's hunger and not his stomach's hunger. When an individual is hungry, not only is his stomach growling, but other areas of him are affected. His perceptions change (he will perceive food more readily than he will at other times); his memory changes (he is apt to remember a good meal at this time more than at others); his emotions change (he is more tense and nervous than at other times); the content of his thinking changes (he is more apt to thing about getting food than solving math problems). When Bert Nemcik is hungry, he is hungry all over and not just in his stomach (p. 20).

2.   Hunger as Paradigm

The common assumption is that all drives follow the example set by physiological drives. Most drives cannot be isolated from one another. The typical human desire is a need of the whole person. It is important for the individual to accept the interrelatedness of the separate but not unique drives present within the self. The hunger drive which seems so simple when compared to the drive for love is actually not so simple in the end (Goldstein, 1939). The motivation researcher faced with the choice of dealing with either (1) experimentally simple problems that are trivial or invalid, or

(2) experimental problems that are fearfully difficult but important, the choice needs to be the latter (p. 21).

3.   Means and Ends

In examining daily living, desires are usually a means to an end rather than an end in themselves. Earning money is necessary for an individual who wants to purchase a car. Money is the means to the end. Studying symptoms is not so important as placing them in some overall context. A deeper analysis into what goals or needs are behind what drives the individual leads to a greater understanding of what motivates people. Conscious motivational behaviors cannot explain unconscious ones. Psychoanalysis demonstrates that ultimate unconscious aims need not be direct at all. Sound motivation theory must consider the unconscious life as well in order to connect the inner and external means that produce a desired end (p. 21).

4.   Desire and Culture

Anthropological evidence indicates that fundamental desires of all human beings do not differ nearly as much as do their conscious everyday desires. Two different cultures may provide completely different means to satisfy a particular desire. Maslow (1954) described how self-esteem in one society might be fulfilled by becoming a good hunter, while in another, the individual would become a great warrior. The dynamics are the same. Ends are more universal than the roads taken to achieve them.

5.   Multiple Motivations

Psychopathology research indicates that a conscious desire or motivated behavior is allied with another and serves as a channel through which other purposes may express themselves. For example, sexual behavior and conscious sexual desires may be tremendously different in their underlying, unconscious purposes. The sexual desire may have the same content in individuals, but we know this to be inaccurate. This holds true for both preparatory and consummatory sexual behavior. Maslow (1954) emphasized that it is unusual that an act or conscious wish have but one motivation (p. 23).

6.   Motivating States

Static psychology would be satisfied to analyze what a person is feeling, say, depressed, and put a period to this assessment. Dynamic psychology would attempt to imply that many things are involved in this feeling of depression. This feeling causes repercussions in all parts of the organism. There may be tension, strain, and unhappiness as a result. The feeling may prompt many behavioral responses. The feeling of depression is a self motivating state. Maslow (1970) believed motivational theory should assume that it is a constant, never ending, fluctuating, and complex organismic state of being (p. 24).

7.   Relationships and Motivations

According to Maslow (1979) human beings are a "wanting animal" and rarely reach a state of complete satisfaction except for a short period time. Once one desire is satisfied another arises to take its place. Throughout life, humans are always desiring something. The appearance of the drive or desire and the actions that it arouses and the satisfaction that comes from attaining the goal, all taken together, give the individual only an isolated instance taken out of the total complex of the human motivational unit. Thus, motivation depends on the state of satisfaction or dissatisfaction present within the human being. Wanting something else, according to Maslow, implies that there is an already existing satisfaction of other wants. The starving artist will not paint much when his stomach is growling.

Many motivational theorists pay little attention to the fact that the human being is never satisfied except in a one-step-along-the-path fashion and wants seem to arrange themselves in some sort of hierarchy of need.

8.   List of Drives

Lists of drives and needs are unsound motivational theory. They imply an equality of the various drives that are listed. Secondly, they imply each is isolated from the other. Thirdly, these lists are usually based purely on behavior neglecting completely all that is known about the nature of drives. There is no arithmetic progression from one to another. Rather, they arrange themselves in a hierarchy of needs, with the lowest progressing toward the highest which is self actualization. There is no mutual exclusiveness between drives, Maslow (1970) wrote, but an overlapping which blurs any simple recognition of one being different from another. When referring to physiological needs, it is easy to separate instigation from the goal object. But it is not easy to distinguish the drive and goal object from the drive when dealing with the desire of love. The drive and the desire, the goal object, seem to be the same thing but are distinctly different (p. 26).

9.   Classification of Motivational Life

Maslow (1970) believed that the only basis on which any classification of motivational life can be constructed is that of the fundamental goals or needs rather than on any listing of drives. Only the fundamental goals remain constant through all the flux that a dynamic approach forces upon psychology theorizing. Motivating behavior is not a sound basis for classification because there are too many variables which affect such activity. An individual going through the whole process of sexual desire, courting behavior, and consummatory love making may actually be seeking self-esteem rather than sexual gratification. Only by a process of logical exclusion are we able to isolate goals or needs as the foundation for classification in motivation theory (Murray, 1938).

10.   Motivation and Animal Data

Researchers have relied largely on animal experiments in developing theories of motivation. White rats are not human beings and therefore, some of the research that theories have been based on are not accurate for humans. As we go up the phyletic scale, instincts begin to disappear and appetites become more important and hungers less. As instincts begin to drop away, there is more emphasis and dependence on culture as an adaptive tool. In order to use any animal data, we must realize that we are much more like primates (monkeys) than white rats (Harlow, 1953; Harlow, 1960; Harlow, 1962; Harlow, 1964; Harlow & Harlow, 1965; Harlow & Harlow, 1966; Howells & Vine, 1940).

11.   Environment

Human motivation rarely actualizes itself in behavior except in relation to the situation and to other people. Any theory of motivation must take into consideration environment, the organism, and the role of cultural determination. Maslow (1970) cautioned the theorizer from going to extremes. The individual partly creates the barrier which impedes him from achieving his need, want, or goal. For instance, the child who struggles to attain a certain object of value to him and is restrained by some barrier, determines not only that the object is of value, but also that the barrier is abarrier. Psychologically, there is no such thing as a barrier; there is only a barrier for a particular person who is trying to get something that he wants. Sound motivation theory, according to Maslow, must take into account the situation, but must never become pure situational theory. Unless we are willing to give up a search for an understanding of the nature of the constancy of the organism in favor of understanding the world it lives in, we will not achieve any fully functional theory of motivation (p. 29).

12.   Integration

Motivation theory must take into account that the organism behaves ordinarily as an integrated whole and sometimes it does not. The organism seems to be most unified when it is successfully facing either a great joy or creative moment, or when it is facing a major problem or threat or emergency situation. Due to our lack of ignorance or our ability to understand the whole person, we sometimes are incapable of deciding which part of the individual is controlling the whole. It is becoming clear now, that such functioning is not necessarily to be regarded as evidence of weak, bad, or pathological motivations. Rather, it is to be regarded as evidence of one of the most important capacities of the organism: the ability to deal with problems in a partial, specific, or segmental fashion so that the main capacities of the organism are still left free for the more important and more challenging problems it will face (Goldstein, 1939).

13.   Non-motivated Behavior

Not all behaviors or reactions are motivated by some seeking for what is lacked or needed. The phenomenon of maturation, of expression, and of growth or self-actualization are all instances of exceptions to this rule of universal motivation. Maier (1939) proposed that most neurotic symptoms or trends amount to basic need-gratification-bent impulses that have somehow been stymied or misdirected or confused with other needs or fixated on the wrong means.

They have no goal but to prevent further hurt, threat, or frustration. Maier (1949) believed the difference is like that between the fighter who still hopes to win and the one who has no hope of winning, but tries only to lose as painfully as possible. Klee (1951) wrote that since giving up and hopelessness are definitely of considerable relevance to prognosis in therapy, to expectations of learning, even to longevity, all these facets of human behavior must be considered in any definitive motivation theory.

14.   Possibility of Attainment

Dewey (1939) and Thorndike (1940) stressed one important aspect of motivation that was completely neglected by most psychologists, namely, possibility. Humans yearn for that which might conceivably be attained. We are much more realistic about wishing than the psychoanalysts might allow, absorbed as they are with unconscious wishes. Attention to this factor of possibility of attainment is crucial for understanding the differences in motivations between various classes within our own population and between it and other poorer countries and cultures.

15.   Influence of Reality

For Freud (1933) an id impulse is a discrete entity having no intrinsic relatedness to anything else in the world, not even to other id impulses:

> We can come nearer to the id with images, and call it a chaos, a cauldron of seething excitement....These instincts fill it with energy, but it has no organization and no unified will, only an impulsion to obtain satisfaction for the instinctual needs, in accordance with the pleasure principle. The law of logic--above all, the law of contradiction--do not hold for processes in the id. Contradictory impulses exist side by side

without neutralizing each other or drawing apart; at most they combine in compromise formations under the empowering economic pressure towards discharging their energy. There is nothing in the id which can be compared to negation, and we are astonished to find it in an exception to the philosopher's assertion that space and time are necessary formations of our mental acts....Naturally, the id knows no values, no good and evil, no morality. The economic or quantitative factor which is so closely bound up with the pleasure-principle, dominates all its processes. Instinctual catharsis seeking discharge is all that the id contains (pp. 103-105)

Dewey (1940) contended that all impulses, at least in the adult, are integrated with and affected by reality. He maintained that there are no id impulses, and if there are, they are intrinsically pathological rather than intrinsically healthy.

Maslow (1970) noted the contradiction between the two authors and asked, at what point in the life history does the infantile fantasy begin to be modified by a perception of reality? Is it the same for all, neurotic and healthy alike? Can the efficiently functioning human being maintain completely free of such influence any hidden corner of his impulse life? Or if it does turn out that such impulses do exist in all of us, when do they appear, under what conditions, and must they be in opposition to reality? (p. 33).

16.   Knowledge of Healthy Motivation

The motivational life of neurotic sufferers should be rejected as a paradigm for healthy motivation. Any theory of motivation that is worthy of attention must begin with the highest capacities of the healthiest, strongest human beings as well as the defensive maneuvers of crippled spirits (Maslow, 1970, p. 33).

Maslow's work involved an attempt to answer many of the questions raised above in these 16 points. He wanted to evaluate the nature of human motivation from all perspectives. His enquiries set the stage for the development of the first inclusive theory which contained holistic concepts that enhanced the image of mankind in the context of the human condition of life.

10. MASLOW'S THEORY OF HUMAN MOTIVATION

Maslow (1970) formulated a positive theory of motivation that he believed would satisfy the theoretical demands listed in the 16 principles listed above. Most of his work resulted directly from clinical experience. He believed his theory was founded in the functionalist tradition of Dewey and James, and was fused with the holism of Wertheimer, Goldstein, Gestalt Therapy, the dynamicism of Freud, Fromm, Horney, Reich, Jung, and Adler. He labeled this integration or synthesis a "holistic-dynamic theory."

Physiological Needs

Most motivation theories begin with the physiological drives. Recent research makes it necessary to revise traditional notions about needs: first, the development of the concept of homeostasis, and second, the finding that appetites (preferential choices among foods) are a fairly efficient indication of actual needs or lacks in the body.

Homeostasis refers to the body's automatic efforts to maintain a constant or normal state of the blood stream. Cannon (1932) described this process for (1) the water content of the blood, (2) salt content, (3)sugar content, (4) protein content, (5) fat content, (6) calcium content, (7) oxygen content, (8) constant hydrogen-ion level (acid base balance), and (9) constant temperature of the blood.

Young (1948; 1941) summarized the work on appetite and its relation to body needs. He theorized that if the body lacks some chemical, the individual will tend to develop a specific appetite or partial hunger for that missing food element. It is impossible to make any list of fundamental physiological needs for they can come to almost any number one might wish, depending on the degree of specificity of description. What this means is that the person missing everything in life in an extreme fashion will most likely be motivated to satisfy physiological needs rather than any others. If a person is lacking food, safety, love, and esteem, he would hunger for food more strongly than for anything else. For the person who is extremely or dangerously hungry, no other interests exist but food. He dreams food, remembers food, perceives food, and wants only food. All other drives are stifled, including sex, and a pure hunger drive exists.

One peculiar characteristic of the human organism is that when it is dominated by a certain need, its whole philosophy of the future tends also to change. Utopia for the chronically hungry man would be a place where there is plenty of food. Life itself tends to be defined in terms of eating. Anything else in life is unimportant. Freedom, love, community feeling, respect, philosophy, may all seem useless since they fail to fill the stomach. The average American citizen is experiencing appetite rather than hunger when he says, "I am hungry." He may experience sheer life-and-death hunger only by accident and then only a few times throughout his entire life.

Maslow (1970) maintained that "it is quite true that man lives by bread alone - when there is no bread." But what happens to man's desires when there is plenty of bread and when his belly is filled? It is then that other higher needs emerge and these, rather than physiological hungers, dominate the organism. When these are satisfied, again new and still higher needs emerge, and so on. This is what Maslow meant when he wrote that human needs are organized into a hierarchy of "relative prepotency."

In his theory, gratification is as important as deprivation. Once a need is met, the organism is released from the domination of physiological needs, thus, permitting the emergence of other more social goals. A want that is satisfied is no longer a want. Maslow hypothesized that in individuals in whom a certain need has always been satisfied are best equipped to tolerate deprivation of that need in the future. Those who have been deprived in the past will react differently to current satisfactions than the those who have never been deprived.

Safety Needs

Once physiological needs are gratified, then there emerges a new set of needs which Maslow (1970) categorized as safety needs: security; stability; dependency; protection; freedom from fear, from anxiety and chaos; need for structure, order, law, limits; strength in the protector. A man whose hunger is satisfied but feels unsafe, if it is extreme and chronic enough, may be characterized as living almost for safety alone.

The average child, and less obviously, the average adult generally prefers a safe, orderly, predictable, lawful, organized world which he can count on and in which unexpected, unmanageable, chaotic, or other dangerous things do not happen, and in which he has powerful parents or protectors who shield him from harm. The healthy and fortunate adult in American society is largely satisfied in his safety needs. The peaceful, smoothly running, stable, good society ordinarily makes its members feel safe enough from wild animals, extremes of temperature, criminal assault, murder, chaos, and tyranny. When Maslow first proposed his theory in 1954 and the revised work in 1970, crime in

American streets was largely confined to certain areas. In the past five years, the safety need is becoming more of an issue. As of January 12, 1994, 12 murders were committed in Washington, D.C., our nation's capital, in the first 12 days of the new year. Violence in our neighborhoods, communities, and cities will surely become a major safety issue if it continues to proliferate in the last six years of this decade.

Other aspects of the attempt to seek safety and stability in the world are seen in the very common preference for familiar rather than unfamiliar things, or for the known rather than the unknown (Maslow, 1937). The tendency to use religion or philosophy to organize the universe and man into it in some sort of coherent, meaningful whole is motivated by the safety need. The need for safety is an active and dominant mobilizer of the human's resources only in real emergencies. Some neurotic adults are like unsafe children in their desire for safety. The neurotic individual may be described with great usefulness as a grown-up person who retains his childhood attitudes toward the world. A neurotic adult behaves as if he were actually afraid of being spanked, or denied his mother's approval, or having his food taken away from him. His childish attitudes of fear and threat reaction to the dangerous world go underground. Untouched by the growing up and learning processes, this individual can be affected by any stimulus that feels threatening (Horney, 1937).

The neurosis in which the search for safety takes its clearest form is in the compulsive-obsessive. These individuals try frantically to order and stabilize the world so that no unmanageable, unexpected, or unfamiliar dangers will ever appear. They develop all sorts of ceremonials, rules, and formulas so that every possible contingency may be provided for and so that no new contingencies may appear. They are like brain-injured cases who manage to maintain equilibrium by avoiding everything unfamiliar and strange and by ordering their restricted world in such a neat, disciplined fashion that everything in the world can be counted on (Goldstein, 1939).

The safety needs can become very urgent on the social scene whenever there are real threats to law and order, to the authority of society. The conditions in many cities today (1994) with the exponential increase in violent crime has caused the issue of gun access and gun control to become an extremely heated debate. Though most Americans will never be violently assaulted due to the sheer odds, many people feel the compulsion to arm themselves with handguns and assault weapons capable of discharging 15-30 rounds of ammunition semi-automatically. Domestic violence in families significantly increased in the last decade. This, coupled with the rise in street crime, makes the issue of safety a compelling one for many Americans. The threat of chaos, or of nihilism, can be expected in many human beings to produce a regression from any higher needs to the more prepotent safety needs.

A common reaction in such situations is the acceptance of a dictatorship or of a military style rule. With the breakup of the Soviet Block Nations and the movement toward a free economy system in Russia, a concomitant rise in crime is occurring. On NBC News (January 12, 1994), Tom Brokaw, reporting from Moscow, profiled the rapid development of a "Russian Mafia" which accounted for over 200 murders in that city in the past year alone. At the same time, there is a rising debate over the necessity to return to the old ways, the old Bolshevik controls, in order to stem the tide of violence and crime in the new Russia.

All human beings respond to danger with realistic regression to the safety need level, and will prepare to defend themselves in any manner that seems necessary to thwart the danger. Turning the cheek may be biblically correct, but in reality, "Do unto others first before they do unto you" rules the street corner today. Most people living near the edge of the safety line, are disturbed by threats to legality, and to the representatives of the law who seem to be incapable of protecting them from harm.

The Belongingness and Love Needs

Once physiological and safety needs are met, there emerges the need for belongingness, love, and affection. The cycle of needs satisfaction repeats itself, and this new need becomes the epicenter of his life. A human being will feel the absence of friends, or wife or children. He will hunger for affectionate relationships with people in general, and for a place in his group or family. He will feel the pangs of loneliness, of ostracism, of rejection, of friendliness, of rootlessness (Maslow, 1959).

There is little scientific information about the belongingness need, although there is a common theme in novels, poems, plays, and autobiographies. From these, we know in a general way the destructive effects on children of moving too often, of disorientation, of the general over-mobility that is forced by industrialization, of being without roots, or of despising one's roots, one's origins, one's group, of being torn from one's home and family friends and neighbors (Maslow, 1970).

We still underplay the deep importance of the neighborhood, of one's territory, of one's clan, of one's own kind. In Ardrey's (1966) <u>Territorial Imperative</u>, with great poignancy and conviction, he described the need for the individual to belong to something, to someone, our deep animal tendency to herd.

In our society, the thwarting of the belongingness and love needs is found in the core cases of maladjustment and severe pathology. Love and affection are looked upon with ambivalence and are sometimes hedged about with many restrictions and inhibitions. Many clinical studies have assessed this need, and like Suttie (1935) concluded that within our culture there exists a "taboo on tenderness."

Maslow (1970) stressed that love is not synonymous with sex, and sex is a purely physiological need and is multi-determined. He maintained that the tremendous growth in T-groups and other personal growth groups and intentional communities may be motivated by an unsatisfied hunger for contact, for intimacy, for belongingness. He hypothesized that some proportion of youth rebellion groups may be motivated by the profound hunger for groupiness. Spergel and Chance (1991) supported this notion in their research on youth gangs in America concluding that "belonging to something was better than not belonging to anything. The gang, unlike the modern American family, provides support, a sense of community, and basically, protection. If a family or a society cannot satisfy this need, then the gang will."

The Esteem Need

All people need a stable, firmly based, high evaluation of themselves. Self-respect, self-esteem, and the esteem of others is necessary for an individual to feel whole. These needs are manifested in a desire for strength, for achievement, for adequacy, for mastery and competence, for confidence in the face of the challenges of the world. Satisfaction of the self-esteem need leads to a feeling of self-confidence, worth, strength, capability, and adequacy, of being useful, and necessary in the world (Adler, 1939; 1964).

Thwarting these needs produces feelings of inferiority, of weakness, and of helplessness. They in turn give rise to either basic discouragement or else compensatory or neurotic trends. An appreciation of the necessity of basic self-confidence and an understanding of how helpless people are without it can be gained from a study of severe traumatic neurosis (Kardiner, 1941).

From the theologians' discussion of pride and hubris, from the Frommian theories about the self-perception of untruth to one's own nature, from the Rogerian work with self, from essayists like Ayn Rand (1943), we learn more and more about the dangers of basing self-esteem on the opinions of others rather than on real capacity, competence, and adequacy to the task. The most stable and healthy self-esteem is based on deserved respect from others rather than on external fame or celebrity and unwarranted adulation. It is helpful to distinguish the actual competence and achievement that is based on sheer will power, determination and responsibility, from that which comes naturally and easily out of one's own true inner nature, one's constitution, one's biological fate or destiny, or as Horney (1950) put it, "out of the REAL SELF rather than out of the idealized pseudo-self.

The Need for Self-Actualization

Even if the first four needs are satisfied, the human being will still develop a restlessness, a discontent, unless the individual is doing what he, individually, is fitted for. A musician must make music, a teacher teach, a poet write poems, a bricklayer lay bricks, if he is to ultimately be at peace with himself. What a man can be, he must be. He must be true to his own nature. This need Maslow (1954) called self-actualization.

First coined by Goldstein (1940), self-actualization refers to a man's desire for self-fulfillment, or to become actualized in what he is potentially. This tendency might be phrased the desire to become more and more what one idiosyncratically is, to become everything that one is capable of becoming. What form this takes varies from person to person. The clear emergence of these needs usually follows the satisfaction of the physiological, safety, love and esteem needs. Of the five needs defined in Maslow's hierarchy, this last one is the most difficult to fulfill, and is the most sought after of them all.

In my work with new employees beginning their work experience with the Abraxas Foundation, I find all these needs in effect. Needing to work in order to survive, an individual seeks employment with the Foundation. He applies for a position, is interviewed and then returns to his home to wait for a call from the director who needs to fill a position. In the process, he may feel unsafe, unwanted, certainly less than self-actualized. Then one day he receives a phone call from the Human Resources Director to inform him that he has a position with the Foundation and told when to report to work. At that moment, he feels wanted, needed, and self-actualized. He will be able to provide for himself and for his family. He will be safe from the throes of the poverty line. He will feel this way until he reports for his first day of work and begins the new employee orientation process. Everything he knew before, experienced before, believed he understood before, is challenged and the momentary elation of feeling self-actualized evaporates and he must struggle to adapt to a new work environment, a new life situation. Eventually, with guidance and support, with experience, and with a significant amount of effort on his part, he will eventually feel self-actualized again. When and how remains within his own province.

It will happen only if the other basic four needs are consistently met. There will be vacillation through time. Self-actualization may come easily to some and more difficultly to others. The human condition is unpredictable. Events will affect the pace at which the individual satisfies the hierarchy of needs.

Preconditions for Basic Need Satisfactions

Freedom of speech, freedom to do as one pleases, freedom to investigate and seek information, freedom to defend oneself, justice, fairness, honesty, and orderliness, when thwarted, will result in the individual's reacting as if threatened. The individual will defend these freedoms because without them the basic satisfactions are quite impossible.

An act is psychologically important if it contributes to the satisfaction of basic needs. A similar statement may be made for the various defense or coping mechanisms. Some are directly related to the protection or attainment of the basic needs. Others are only weakly related. Any danger to the more basic defense mechanisms is more threatening than danger to less basic defenses.

Motivation to Know and Understand

Maslow (1970) maintained that the reason we know little about the cognitive impulses that motivate human beings is that they are not important in the clinic. The exciting and mysterious symptoms found in the classical neuroses are lacking here. Consequently, we find little on the subject in the writings of the great inventors of psychotherapy and psychodynamics, Freud, Adler, Jung, etc.

Among the academics, Murphy (1958), Wertheimer (1959), and Asch (1952) treated the problem of motivation. Acquiring knowledge and systematizing the universe have been considered techniques for the achievement of basic safety in the world, or for the intelligent man, expressions of self-actualization. Though their formulations may be useful, they did not formulate any definitive answers to the questions as to the motivational role of curiosity, learning, philosophizing, experimenting, etc. in the human being.

Beyond these negative determinants for acquiring knowledge, there are some reasonable grounds for postulating positive impulses to satisfy curiosity, to know, to explain, and to understand (Maslow, 1968). Maslow listed the following conditions under which positive impulses lead to a measure of self-actualization:

1. Something like human curiosity can easily be observed in animals. Monkeys will pick things apart, will poke their fingers into holes, will explore all sorts of situations where it is improbable that hunger, fear, sex, comfort, status, etc. are involved. Harlow's (1950) experiments amply demonstrated this.

2. The history of mankind supplies us with a satisfactory number of instances in which man looked for facts and created explanations in the face of the greatest danger, even to life itself (Maslow, 1957).

3. Studies of psychologically healthy people indicate that they are attracted to the mysterious, to the unknown, to the chaotic, unorganized, and unexplained. This seems to be an attractiveness. These areas are in themselves and of their own right interesting. The contrasting reaction to the well know is one of boredom (Maslow, 1957).

4. It may be valid to extrapolate from the psychopathological. The compulsive-obsessive neurotic, Goldstein's brain-injured soldiers, Maier's (1939) fixated rats, all show a compulsive and anxious clinging to the familiar and a dread of the unfamiliar, anarchic, the unexpected, the un-domesticated. There are some phenomena that may turn out to nullify this possibility. Among those forced unconventionality, a chronic rebellion against any authority whatsoever, Bohemianism, the desire to shock and to startle, all of which may be found in certain neurotic individuals, as well as in the process of de-acculturation.

5. The needs to know and to understand are seen in late infancy and childhood, perhaps even more strongly than in adulthood. This seems to be a spontaneous product of maturation rather than learning. Children do not have to be taught to be curious. But they **may** be taught, as by institutionalization, **not** to be curious (Goldfarb, 1945).

6.   Finally, the gratification of the cognitive impulses is subjectively satisfying and yields to end-experiences. Though this aspect of insight and understanding has been neglected in favor of achieved results, learning remains true to insight and is usually a bright, happy, emotional spot in a person's life. Perhaps, it can even be viewed as a high spot in the life span (Maslow, 1969).

The Aesthetic Needs

Aesthetic needs are the least researched of all human needs. Maslow (1967) was convinced that, from his clinical observations, some individuals truly possess an aesthetic need. "They get sick from ugliness," he wrote, "and are cured by beautiful surroundings. They crave actively, and their cravings can be satisfied only by beauty" (p. 93). It is seen almost universally in healthy children. Evidence of aesthetic need impulse is found in every culture and in every age as far back as the cave man.

Overlapping aesthetic needs with cognitive needs makes it difficult to separate them. The needs for order, for symmetry, for closure, for completion of the act, for system, and for structure may be indiscriminately assigned to either cognitive or aesthetic, or even to neurotic needs. Maslow asked, "what does it mean when a man feels a strong conscious impulse to straighten the crookedly hung picture on the wall?" Is it conative, cognitive, or aesthetic? This is a research question which still needs to be asked and studied in greater detail to determine which is the most accurate one.

Maslow (1970) contended that the hierarchy of needs is not nearly so rigid as he may have implied earlier. People seem to have these basic needs in about the order that has been indicated. There are a number of exceptions:

1.   For some people, self-esteem seems to be more important than love. This common reversal in the hierarchy is usually due to the development of the notion that the person who is most likely to be loved is a strong or powerful person, one who inspires respect or fear and who is self-confident or aggressive.

2.   There are other innately creative people in whom the drive to creativeness seems to be more important than any other counterdeterminant. This creativeness appears not as self-actualization released by basic satisfaction, but in spite of a lack of it.

3.   In certain people the level of aspiration may be permanently deadened or lowered. The less prepotent goals may simply be lost, and may disappear forever so that the person who has experienced life at a very low level never experiences self-actualization.

4.   The so-called psychopathic personality is another example of permanent loss of the love needs. These are people who have been starved for love in the earliest months of their lives and have simply lost forever the desire and the ability to give and to receive affection.

5.   Another cause of reversal of the hierarchy is that when a need has been satisfied for a long time, this need may be underevaluated. People who have never experienced chronic hunger are apt to underestimate its effects and to look upon food as a rather unimportant thing. Thus a man who has given up his job rather than lose his

self-respect, and who then starves six months or so, may be willing to take his job back even at the price of losing his self-respect.

6.   Another partial explanation of apparent reversals is seen in the fact that we have been talking about the hierarchy of prepotency in terms of consciously felt wants or desires rather than of behavior. Looking at behavior itself may give us the wrong impression. Looking at behavior itself may give us the wrong impression. What we have claimed is that the person will want the more basic of two needs when deprived in both. There is no necessary implication here that he will act upon his desires (Maslow, 1970, pp. 52-53).

Multiple Determinants of Behavior

Not all behavior is determined by basic needs. Maslow (1970) contended that not all behavior is motivated. There are many determinants of behavior other than motives. One other important class of determinants is the external field. Behavior may be determined completely by the external field, or even by specific, isolated, external stimuli, as in association of ideas, or certain conditioned reflexes. Secondly, some behavior is highly motivated and other behavior is only weakly motivated. Some is not motivated at all. Another important point is that there is a basic difference between expressive and coping behavior. An expressive behavior does not try to do anything; it is simply a reflection of the personality. A stupid man behaves stupidly, not because he wants to, but simply because he is what he is. The random movements of a healthy child, the smile on the face of a happy man even when he is alone, the springiness of the healthy man's walk, and the erectness of his carriage are other examples of expressive, nonfunctional behavior. The style in which a man carries out almost all his behavior, motivated as well as unmotivated, is often most expressive (Allport & Vernon, 1933; Wolff, 1943).

The chief principle of organization in human motivational life is the arrangement of basic needs in a hierarchy of less or greater priority or potency. The chief dynamic principle animating this organization is the emergence in the healthy person of less potent needs upon gratification of the more potent ones. The physiological needs, when unsatisfied, dominate the organism, pressing all capacities into their service and organizing these capacities so that they may be most efficient in this service. Relative gratification submerges them and allows the next higher set of needs in the hierarchy to emerge, dominate, and organize the personality, so that instead of being hunger obsessed, it now becomes safety obsessed. The principle is the same for the other set needs in the hierarchy, for instance, love, esteem, and self-actualization (Maslow, 1935).

Learning and Basic Need Gratification

In general gratification theory, any loss of appetite after satiation, the change in quantity of type and defensiveness after safety need gratification demonstrate:

1.   disappearance with increased exercise, and

2.   disappearance with increased reward (Maslow, 1959, p. 145).

The task of need gratification is almost entirely limited to intrinsically appropriate satisfiers. There can be no casual and arbitrary choice, except for nonbasic needs. For the love-hungry, there is only one genuine, long-run satisfier, honest and satisfying affection. For the sex-starved, food-starved, or water-starved person, only sex, food, or water will ultimately serve. This is the sort of intrinsic appropriateness stressed by Werthheimer (1959), Kohler (1938), and other Gestalt psychologists, such as Asch, Arnheim, Katona, as a central concept in all fields of psychology.

Even in Gestalt learning theory character traits are not considered to be wholly learned. This theory is too limited in its rationalistic stress on the cognition of intrinsic motivation in the outside world. A stronger tie to the conative and affective processes within a person than is afforded either by associative or Gestalt learning is needed (Lewin, 1935).

What can be described as character or intrinsic learning takes place at its centering point changes in the character structure rather than in behavior. Among its many components are the:

1. educative effects of unique (non-repetitive) and of profound personal experiences;

2. affective changes produced by repetitive experiences;

3. conative changes produced by gratification-frustration experiences;

4. broad attitudinal, expectational, or even philosophical changes produced by certain types of early experience; and,

5. determination by constitution of the variation in selective assimilation of any experience by the organism (Levy, 1934, pp. 203-234).

Such considerations point to a closer relationship between the concepts of learning and character formation. It may be productive to define paradigmatic learning as change in personal development, in character, structure, as movement toward self-actualization, and beyond (Maslow, 1969a; Maslow, 1969b; Maslow, 1969c).

The Concept of Gratification Health

If person **A** lived for several weeks in a dangerous jungle where he has managed to stay alive by finding occasional food and water, he would be fulfilling survival needs. Person **B** not only stays alive but also has a rifle and a hidden cave with a closable entrance. Person **C** has all these and two more men with him as well. Person **D** has the food, the gun, the allies, the cave, and in addition, has with him his best-loved friend. Finally, Person **E** has all these and in addition is the well-respected leader of his band. We may call these men, respectively, the merely surviving, the safe, the belonging, the loved, and the respected.

This is not only a series of increasing basic need gratifications, but is a series of increasing degrees of psychological health (Erikson, 1959; Freud, 1920). A man who is safe, belongs, and is loved will be healthier than a man who is safe and belongs, but who feels rejected and unloved. If he wins respect and admiration, and develops self-respect, then he is still more healthy, self-actualizing, and fully human.

Basic need gratification is positively correlated with the degree of psychological health. Gratification theory would suggest that such a correlation of basic needs and good health exists synergistically (Maslow, 1969). It is a general clinical finding that the human being, when fed steady doses of safety, love, respect, he or she works better, perceives more efficiently, uses intelligence more fully, thinks to correct conclusions more often, digests food more efficiently, and is less subject to various diseases (p. 92).

The study of the self-actualizing man indicates the special status of basic human needs. On the satisfaction of these needs is the healthy life based. Self-actualizing individuals are readily seen to be impulse-accepting as the instinct hypothesis would demand rather than impulse-rejecting or repressing (p. 93).

The basic needs arrange themselves in a definite hierarchy on the basis of the principle of relative potency. The safety need is stronger than the love need because it dominates the organism in various ways when both needs are frustrated. The physiological needs are stronger then the safety needs, which are stronger than the love needs, which are stronger than the esteem needs, which are stronger than those needs called, the need for self-actualization.

Maslow (1970) presented the following continuum to explain this hierarchical structure:

1. The higher need is a later phyletic or evolutionary development.

2. Higher needs are later ontogenetic developments.

3. The higher the need the less imperative it is for sheer survival, the longer gratification can be postponed, and the easier it is for the need to disappear permanently.

4. Living at the higher need level means greater biological efficiency, greater longevity, less disease, better sleep, appetite, etc.

5.   Higher needs are less urgent subjectively.

6.   Higher need gratification produce more desirable subjective results, i.e., more profound happiness, serenity, and richness of the inner life.

7.   Pursuit and gratification of higher needs represent a general healthy trend away from psychopathology.

8.   The higher needs have more preconditions.

9.   Higher needs require better outside conditions to make them possible.

10.   A greater value is usually placed upon the higher need than upon the lower by those who have been gratified in both.

11.   The higher the need level, the wider is the circle of love identification, the greater is the number of people love-identified with, and the greater is the average degree of love identification.

12.   The pursuit and the gratification of the higher needs have desirable civic and social consequences.

13.   Satisfaction of higher needs is closer to self-actualization than is lower-need satisfaction.

14.   The pursuit and gratification of the higher needs leads to greater, stronger, and truer individualism.

15.   The higher the need level the easier and more effective psychotherapy can be.

16. The lower needs are far more localized, more tangible, and more limited than the higher needs (p. 100).

The recognition that man's best impulses are appreciably intrinsic and have tremendous implication for motivational theory. It means that it is no longer necessary or desirable to deduce values by logic or to try to read them off from authorities or revelations. Human nature carries within itself the answer to the questions, how can I be good; how can I be fruitful? The human organism tells us what it needs, and thereby, what it values, by sickening when deprived of these values and by growing when not deprived.

Healthy People and the Condition of Self-Actualization.

Healthy people can accept their own human nature with all its shortcomings, discrepancies, and variations from the ideal. They accept themselves without chagrin or complaint, or even without thinking about the matter very much. They can take the foibles, sins, goods and evils of human nature in the same unquestioning spirit with which they accept the characteristics of nature. Their eyes see what is before them without being strained through spectacles of various sorts to distort or shape or color the reality (Bergson, 1944).

What healthy people do feel guilty about are the discrepancies between what is and what might very well be or ought to be. They do not feel bad or guilty about:

1. Improbable shortcomings, e.g., laziness, thoughtlessness, loss of temper, hurting others;

2. Stubborn remnants of psychological ill health, e.g., prejudice, jealousy, envy;

3. Habits, which, though relatively independent of character structure, may yet be very strong, or

4. Shortcomings of the species or of the culture or of the group with which they identified themselves (Adler, 1939; Bergson, 1944; Horney, 1950).

Self-actualizing people can all be described as relatively spontaneous in behavior and in their inner life, thoughts, and impulses. Their behavior is marked by simplicity and naturalness, and by a lack of artificiality or straining for effect. Their unconventionality is not superficial but essential and internal. Recognizing that the world of people in which they live could not understand or accept this, and since they wish no hurt to come to others, they will go through the ceremonies and rituals of convention with a good-humored shrug and with the best possible grace. It is not that they lack conventionality, but that it fits like a cloak that rests very lightly upon their shoulders and they can easily cast it aside thus not permitting it to hamper them. This inner attitude can be seen in moments when they become fully absorbed in something that is close to one of their main interests. They can easily drop off all sorts of rules of behavior to which at other times they conform. It is as if they make a conscious effort to be conventional, as if they were conventional voluntarily and by design. They are often the most ethical of people even though their ethics are not necessarily the same as those of the people around them. Since they are alienated from ordinary conventions and from ordinarily accepted hypocrisies, lies, and inconsistencies of social life, they sometimes feel like spies or aliens in a foreign land, and sometimes behave so. Sometimes they let themselves go deliberately, out of momentary irritation with customary rigidity or with conventional blindness. When trying to teach someone something, they may sometimes find emotions bubbling up from within them that are so pleasant or even ecstatic that it seems almost sacrilegious to suppress them. They are not anxious, guilty, or ashamed of the impression that they make on the onlooker. They claim that they usually behave in a conventional manner because no great issues are involved or because they know people will be hurt or embarrassed by any other kind of behavior. Their ease of penetration to reality, their closer approach to an animal-like or childlike acceptance and spontaneity imply a superior awareness of their own impulses, desires, opinions, and subjective reactions in general (Fromm, 1947; Rand, 1943; Reik, 1943).

Fromm (1941) found that there was a profound difference between self-actualizing people and others; namely, that the motivational life of self-actualizing people is not only quantitatively but also qualitatively different from that of ordinary people. He constructed a different psychology of motivation for self-actualizing people, and called it metamotivation or growth motivation, rather than deficiency motivation. He found that they do not strive in the ordinary sense, but rather develop beyond the normal. They attempt to grow to perfection and to develop more and more fully in their own style. The motivation of ordinary men is a striving for the basic need gratifications that they lack. Self-actualizing people lack none of these gratifications, and yet they have impulses. They work, they try, and they are ambitious, even though in an unusual sense. For them, motivation is just character growth, character expression, maturation, and development, or self-actualization.

Self-actualized people are generally focused on problems outside themselves. They are problem centered rather than ego centered. They generally are not problems for themselves and are not much concerned about themselves as contrasted with ordinary introspectiveness that is finds in insecure people. They customarily have some mission in life, some task to fulfill, some problem outside themselves which enlists much of their energies (Buhler & Mussarik, 1968; Frankl, 1969). They seem never to get so close to the trees that they cannot see the forest. They work within a framework of values that are broad and not petty, universal and not local, and view life in terms of a century rather than the moment. This impression of being above small things, of having a larger horizon, a wider breadth of vision, of living in the widest frame of reference is of the utmost social interpersonal importance.

A unique characteristic of self-actualized people is that they can be solitary without harm to themselves and without discomfort. It seems true that for almost all that they positively like solitude and privacy to a definitely greater degree than the average person. They can remain above the battle, unruffled and undisturbed by that which produces turmoil in others. They retain their dignity even in undignified surroundings and situations. In general, they are more objective than average people. They possess the ability to concentrate to a greater degree than ordinary people. This intense concentration sometimes produces a by-product called absent-mindedness, and the ability to forget and to be oblivious of their surroundings. Physiologically, they sleep soundly, have an undisturbed appetite, are able to smile and laugh through a period of problems, worry, and responsibility. In their silent moments, they pray and are spiritually alive. Self-actualizing people do not need others in the ordinary sense of the word. Thus, it is easily interpreted by "normal" people as coldness, snobbishness, lack of affection, unfriendliness, or even hostility. They are autonomous, self-disciplined, deciding agents rather than pawns in the game of life. Self-actualizing people have more "free will" and are less "determined" than average people are. They are the leaders of the Democratic self-choice society because they are self-movers, self-deciders, self-choosers who make up their own minds without needing the support or the permission of others (Asch, 1956; McClelland, 1961; McClelland, 1964; McClelland & Winter, 1969).

Since they are propelled by growth motivation rather than by deficiency motivation, self-actualizing people are not dependent for their main satisfactions on the real world, other people, the culture, or on extrinsic satisfactions. They are dependent for their own development and continued growth on their own potentialities and latent resources. Being independent of the environment means a relative stability in the face of hard knocks, blows, deprivations, frustrations, and set-backs. They maintain their relative serenity in the midst of circumstances that would drive other people to suicide. Deficiency-motivated people must have other people available, since most of their main need gratifications (love, safety, respect, prestige, belongingness) come only from other human beings. Growth-motivated people actually become hampered by other people. Their determinants for satisfaction and the good life are inner-individual and not social. They are strong enough to be independent of the opinions of other people, or even their affection. They value less the honors, rewards, status, popularity, prestige, and the love they can bestow, than self-development and inner growth (Huxley, 1955; Northrop, 1947; Rand, 1943; Rogers, 1961).

Self-actualizing people possess the wonderful capacity to appreciate the basics of life, with awe, pleasure, wonder, and even ecstasy, however stale these experiences may become to others. Wilson (1969) called this, worship of the "newness of simple things." For such people, any sunset may be beautiful as the first one, any flower as breath-taking as another even after they have seen a million flowers. They remain convinced of their luck in marriage thirty years after their marriage ceremony. For such people, even the casual workday and moment-to-moment business can be thrilling. These intense feelings do not come all the time, but at the most unexpected moments. They may cross a river on the ferry ten times and on the eleventh crossing experience the feelings, reactions to beauty, and excitement as when they rode the ferry for the very first time (Eastman, 1928). It may be that this acute richness of subjective experience is an aspect of closeness of relationship to the concrete and fresh. Staleness of experience is a consequence of ticketing off a rich perception into one or another category as it proves to be no longer advantageous, or useful, or threatening, or otherwise, ego-involved (Bergson, 1944). Herzberg's (1966) studies of "hygiene" factors in industry, Wilson's observations on the St. Neot's margin (1967; 1969) and Maslow's (1965) study of "low grumbles, high grumbles, and metagrumbles" all show that life could be vastly improved if people could count their own blessings as self-actualizing people can and do, and if they can retain their constant sense of good fortune and gratitude for it.

The subjective expressions that James (1943) called "mystic experiences" are common for self-actualized people. These are the same feelings of limitless horizons opening up to the vision, of being simultaneously more powerful, of the great ecstacy and wonder and awe, of the loss of time and space, and finally, the conviction that something extremely important and valuable has happened so that people are transformed and strengthened even in their daily life by such experiences. Many current psychologists call these "peak experiences." The acute mystic or peak experience is a tremendous intensification of any of those in which there is loss of self or transcendence of it like problem centering, intense concentration, mega-behavior and other intense sensuous experiences (Benedict, 1970). Nonspeaking self-actualizers tend to be practical, effective people, mesomorphs living in the world and doing very well in it. Peakers seem to live in the realm of Being; of poetry, esthetics; symbols; transcendence; "religion" of the mystical, personal, noninstitutional sort; and of end-experiences (Laski, 1962; Maslow, 1964; Maslow, 1968; Maslow, 1962, Maslow, 1969).

Gemeinschaftsgefuhl, a word invented by Adler (1939) described the flavor of feelings for mankind expressed by self-actualizing people. They hold for human beings a deep feeling of identification, sympathy, and affection in spite of occasional anger, impatience, or disgust for certain human foibles. They possess a genuine desire to help the human race. They conduct their lives as if they were all members of a single family. Self-actualizing people are different from others in thought, impulse, behavior, and emotion. In basic ways, they are like aliens in a strange land. Few people understand them, however much they are like by others. They are often saddened, exasperated, and even enraged by the shortcomings of the average person. The knowledge that they can do many things better than the average person, that they can see things others cannot, that the truth is so clear to them and for most it is veiled and hidden, is what Adler called the "older-brotherly attitude."

Self-actualizing people maintain deeper and more profound interpersonal relations than other adults. They are capable of more fusion, greater love, more perfect identification, more obliteration of the ego boundaries than other people would consider possible. A downside to this is that self-actualizing people have deep ties with few individuals. Their circle of friends is small. The ones that they love profoundly are few in number. They have an especially tender love for children and are easily touched by them. In a real sense, they have compassion for all mankind. This love is not indiscriminate. They can and do speak realistically and harshly of those who deserve it, and especially of those who are hypocritical, pretentious, pompous, or self-inflated. The briefest possible description is to say that their hostile reactions to others are deserved, and for the good of the person attacked or for someone else's good. Fromm (1964) maintained that hostility is not character based, but is reactive or situational. Self-actualized people are not susceptible to this human foible.

In the deepest sense, self-actualizing people are democratic people. They are friendly with anyone of suitable character regardless of class, education, political belief, race, or color. They are often not even aware of these differences which are for the average person so obvious and important. They find it possible to learn from anybody who has something to teach them, no matter what other characteristics the others may have. In this learning relationship, they do not try to maintain any outward dignity or to maintain status or age prestige. They are quite aware of how little they know in comparison with what could be known and what is known by others. It is possible for them to be honestly respectful and even humble before people who can teach them something that they do not know or who have a skill they do not possess. Most profound, is their desire to give a certain amount of respect to any human being just because he is a human individual. They are more than less likely to counterattack against evil people and their behaviors. Lastly, they are far less ambivalent, confused, or weak-willed about their own anger than average people are (Fromm, 1964).

In daily living, they demonstrate less chaos and confusion in knowing the difference between right and wrong. They are strongly ethical, and have definite moral standards. Their notions about right and wrong, good and evil, are often not conventional ones. Levy (1951) pointed out that a few centuries ago, these people would have been described as "men who walk in the path of God or as godly men." A few say that they believe in God, but describe this God more as a metaphysical concept than as a personal figure. Self-actualizing people behave as though means and ends are clearly distinguishable. Generally, they are fixed on ends. They make the situation more complex because they regard ends themselves as the many experiences and activities that they are. It is possible for them to make out of the most trivial and routine activity an intrinsically enjoyable game or dance or play. Wertheimer (1961) pointed out that most children are so creative that they can transform hackneyed routine, mechanical, and rote experiences as in experiments, transporting books from one set of shelves to another, into a structured and amusing game of a sort by doing this according to a certain system or with a certain rhythm.

Self-actualized people possess a sense of humor that is not ordinary. They do not consider funny what the average person finds humorous. They do not laugh at others possibly hurting them, nor do they laugh at a smutty joke. They consider humor to be closely allied to philosophy, and generally poke fun at human beings at large when they are foolish, or forget their place in the universe as being abysmally insignificant. Lincoln's humor serves as an example for them in that his jokes never hurt anyone. They may be said to be less humorous than the average in the population. The average person might consider them to be rather on the sober or even serious side. Their humor can be pervasive, and includes the human situation, human pride, seriousness, busy-ness, bustle, ambition, striving and planning. This attitude rubs off on professional work itself, which in a certain sense is also play, and which, though taken seriously, is also taken lightly (Maslow, 1969).

More than any other characteristic, self-actualized people are creative. There is no exception. Each one shows in one way or another a special kind of creativeness or originality or inventiveness. It is not the genius or special-talent creativeness of the Mozart type. Geniuses display a creativity that is not easily understood. The creativeness of self-actualized people seems most like the naive and universal creativeness of unspoiled children. Santayana (1946) called this the "second naivete." This creativeness does not appear in the usual forms of writing books, composing music, or producing artistic objects, but is rather much more humble. It is a special type of creativity, being an expression of a healthy personality and is projected out into the world in whatever activity the person engages in. They become creative shoemakers, carpenters, and clerks. This creativity is manifested in a greater freshness, penetration, and efficiency of perception than the average person. These people are less inhibited, constricted, bound, enculturated than their peers. Likewise, they are more spontaneous, natural, and human. If there were no choking forces in our society, we might expect that all human beings would demonstrate this special type of creativeness (Anderson, 1959; Maslow, 1958).

Self-actualizing people are not well adjusted in the naive sense of approval of and identification with the culture. They get along with the culture in various ways, and all of them may be said to resist enculturation and maintain a certain inner detachment from the culture in which they are immersed (Maslow, 1968).

Reisman (1950) pointed out their resistance to enculturation is a complex issue to unravel. He proposed the following notions as possible explanations for this phenomena:

1. All these people fall within the limits of apparent conventionality in choice of clothes, of language, of food, of ways of doing things in our culture. And yet they are not really conventional, certainly not in the fashionable, chic, or smart ways.

2. None of these people can be called authority rebels in the adolescent or irresponsible sense. They show no active impatience or moment-to-moment, chronic, long-term discontent with the culture or preoccupation with changing it quickly. They often show bursts of indignation with injustice. When quick change is possible or when resolution and courage are needed, it is present in these people.

3. An inner feeling of detachment from the culture is not necessarily conscious but is displayed by almost all, particularly in discussions of the American culture as a whole. They are certainly very different from the ordinary sort person who passively yields to cultural shaping displayed for instance by the ethnocentric subjects of the many studies of authoritarian personalities. Detachment from the culture is probably reflected in self-actualizing subjects' isolation from people and their liking for privacy, which has been described as less important than the average person's need for the familiar and customary.

4.   They are autonomous, ruled by laws of their own character rather than by the rules of society. It is in this sense that they are not merely Americans, but to a greater degree than others, members at large of the human race (p. 33-34).

Reisman asked this question: Is it possible to be a good or healthy man in an imperfect culture? He concluded, that yes, it was possible. These people manage to get along by a complex combination of inner autonomy and outer acceptance that is possible only so long as the culture remains tolerant of this kind of detached withholding from complete cultural identification. This is not ideal health. The imperfect society forces inhibitions and restraints on these people. Since few people can attain health in our culture, those who do attain it are lonely for their own kind (Dembo, 1961).

Self-actualized people possess a wish for perfection and sometimes, their guilt or shame about shortcomings are projected upon various kinds of people from whom the average man demands much more than they themselves give. They are equipped with silly, wasteful, and thoughtless habits. They can be boring and irritating. They are not free from all superficial vanities, pride, partiality to their own productions, family, friends, and children. Temper outbursts are possible. They are also capable of an extraordinary and unexpected ruthlessness. Since they are very strong people, this makes it possible for them to display surgical coldness when this is called for beyond the power of the average man. In their concentration, in their fascinated interest, in their intense concentration on some phenomenon or question, they may become absent-minded or humorless and forget their ordinary social politeness. Even their kindness can lead them into mistakes. Finally, they are not free of guilt, anxiety, sadness, self-castigation, internal strife, and conflict. What Maslow (1970) concluded from this analysis was that "there are no perfect human beings. To avoid disillusionment with human nature, we must first give up our illusions about it" (p. 144).

A firm foundation for a value system is automatically furnished to self-actualized people by their acceptance of the nature of the self, of human nature, of social life and the nature of physical reality. This foundation is supplied to all self-actualized people by their intrinsic dynamics. Among these are:

1.   Their peculiar comfortable relationships with reality;

2.   Their Gemeinschaftsgefuhl;

3.   Their basically satisfied condition from which flow, as epiphenomena, various consequences of surplus, of wealth, overflowing abundance;

4.   Their characteristically discriminating relations to means and ends (Maslow, 1957).

The uppermost portion of the value system of the self-actualized person is entirely unique and character-structure expressive. Self-actualization is actualization of a self, and no two selves are altogether alike. There is only one Renoir, one Brahms, one Spinoza, one John Doe. Though self-actualized individuals have much in common, each is unmistakenly unique. They are more completely individual than any group yet described. They are closer to both humanhood and to their unique individuality.

In conclusion, what has been considered in the past to be polarities or opposites or dichotomies were so only in less healthy people. In healthy people, these dichotomies were resolved, the polarities disappeared, and many opposites thought to be intrinsic merged with each other to form unities (Chenault, 1969).

The dichotomy between selfishness and unselfishness disappears altogether in healthy people because every act is both selfish and unselfish (Maslow, 1964). They are simultaneously very spiritual and very pagan and sensual even to the point where sexuality becomes a path to the spiritual and "religious." Duty cannot be contrasted with pleasure nor work with play when duty is pleasure, when work is play, and the person doing his duty and being virtuous is seeking his pleasure and being happy.

Healthy people are so different from average ones, not only in degree but in kind as well, that they generate two very different kinds of psychology. Maslow (1970) contended that "it becomes more and more clear that the study of crippled, stunted, immature, and unhealthy specimens can yield only a cripple psychology and a cripple philosophy, and the study of self-actualizing people must be the basis for a more universal science of psychology" (p. 180).

Reik (1957) defined love as the absence of anxiety. This is seen with exceptional clearness in healthy individuals. They tend to be more spontaneous, less defensive, less role conscious and strive for intimate relationships. There is less of a tendency to put the best foot forward in a healthy love relationship. In self-actualizing people the quality of the love and sex satisfactions may both improve with the length of the relationship. Generally, self-actualizing love is in part the absence of defenses, and an increase in spontaneity and in honesty. The more a healthy person gets to know the person of the opposite sex, the better he or she will like what is seen.

One of the deepest satisfactions coming from the healthy love relationship is that it permits the greatest spontaneity, the greatest naturalness, the greatest dropping of defenses and protection against threat. Rogers (1951) described this relationship in this way: "Love has here its deepest and most general meaning, and that is of being deeply understood and deeply accepted....We can love a person only to the extent that we are not threatened by him; we can love only if his reactions to us, or to those things which affect us, are understandable to us....Thus, if a person is hostile toward me, and I can see nothing in him at the moment except the hostility, I am quite sure that I will react in a defensive way to the hostility" (p. 159).

Meninger (1942) described the reverse side of the coin. "Love is impaired less by the feeling that we are not appreciated than by a dread, more or less dimly felt by everyone, lest others see through our masks, the masks of repression that have been forced upon us by convention and culture. It is this that leads us to shun intimacy, to maintain friendships on a superficial level, to underestimate and fail to appreciate others lest they come to appreciate us too well" (p. 22).

Self-actualized people were loved and were loving, and are loved and are loving. Psychological health comes from being loved rather than from being deprived of love. They now love and are loved. They have the power to love and the ability to be loved. Though Meninger (1942) made the very acute statement that human beings want to love each other but just don't know how to go about it, this is not true for healthy people. They know how to love, and can do so freely and easily and naturally and without getting wound up in conflicts or threats or inhibitions.

Sex and love are more perfectly fused with each other in healthy people. Although it may be true that these are separate concepts, and although no purpose would be served in confusing them with each other unnecessarily, still it must be reported that in the life of healthy people, they tend to become joined and merged with each other (Reik, 1957; Suttie, 1935).

In self-actualizing people the orgasm is simultaneously more important and less important than in average people. It is often a profound and almost mystical experience, and yet the absence of sexuality is more easily tolerated by these people. This is not a paradox or contradiction. It follows from dynamic motivation theory. Loving at a higher need level makes the lower needs and their frustrations and satisfactions less important, less central, more easily neglected. Schwartz (1951) wrote, "Although totally different in nature, sexual impulse, and love are dependent on and complementary to each other. In a perfect, fully mature human being only this inseparable fusion of sexual impulse and love exists. This is the fundamental principle of any psychology of sex. If there be anyone capable of experiencing the purely physical gratification of sex, he or she is sexually subnormal (immature or otherwise)" (p. 21).

Sexual pleasure in self-actualized people may be very intense or not intense at all. This conflicts with the romantic attitude that love is divine rapture, a transport from the diurnal, a mystical experience. These people do not live on the heights, but usually at a more average level of intensity. Self-actualizing love demonstrates many of the characteristics of self-actualization in general. The acceptance of sexuality is the main basis for the intense enjoyment that these people find in it (Maslow, 1970).

This notion supports D'Arcy's (1947) thesis that erotic and agapean love are basically different but merge in the best people, those that are self-actualized. In healthy people the dichotomies are resolved, and the individual becomes both active and passive, both selfish and unselfish, both masculine and feminine, both self-interested and self-effacing. D'Arcy acknowledged that this occurs though with extreme rarity.

How does self-actualized love manifest itself in the loving couple? The ordinary way in which this need shows itself to the eyes of the world is in terms of taking on responsibility, of care, of concern for another person. The loving husband can get as much pleasure from his wife's pleasure as he can from his own. The loving mother would rather cough herself than hear her child cough. An illness in the good, self-actualized loving couple is an illness of the couple rather than a misfortune of one of the pair. If the relationship is a very good one, the sick or weak one can throw himself upon the care of the protectiveness of the loving partner with the same abandonment and lack of threat and lack of self-consciousness that a child shows in falling asleep in his parent's arms. In less healthy couples, the illness strains the relationship (Maslow, 1970).

Overstreet (1949) stated, "The love of a person implies, not the possession of that person, but the affirmation of that person. It means granting him, gladly, the full right of his unique manhood" (p. 103). The self-actualized man or woman does not pretend to own the other person. The converse is quite true. To own would deny the individual his or her right to be, to become self-actualized. There is no need to own someone else. This would imply a prepotent need that was not fulfilled. Self-actualized love is the highest form of love because it is the free-flowing giving of one person to another without reservations, without pretense, without objections. In this type of relationship, one individual affirms the others individuality, the eagerness for a growth experience for the other, the essential respect for his or her individuality and unique personality. The self-actualizing person will not casually use another or control him or disregard his wishes (p. 104).

Admiration and love in self-actualizing people are most of the time undemanding of rewards and conducive to no purposes, and are experienced in Northrop's (1946) Eastern sense, concretely and richly, for their own sake (Allport, 1961).

It seems healthy people fall in love the way one reacts to one's first appreciative perception of great music: one is awed and overwhelmed by it and loves it. Horney (1950) defined unerotic love in terms of regarding others as ends in themselves rather than means to ends. The consequent reaction is to enjoy, to admire, to be delighted, to contemplate and appreciate, rather than to use. St. Bernard said it very aptly: "Love seeks no cause beyond itself and no limit; it is its own fruit, its own enjoyment. I love because I love; I love in order that I may love..." (Allport, 1947).

Horney (1950) maintained that self-actualizers have no serious deficiencies to make up and must be looked upon as freed for growth, maturation, development, for the fulfillment and actualization of their highest individual and species nature. A paradox seems to be created by the fact that self-actualized people maintain a degree of individuality, of detachment, and autonomy that seems at first glance to be incompatible with the kind of identification and love described above. The fact is that self-actualizing people are simultaneously the most individualistic and the most altruistic and social and loving of all human beings. They can be extremely close to one another and yet go apart when necessary without collapsing. They do not cling to one another. Throughout the most intense and ecstatic love affairs, these people remain themselves, and remain ultimately, the masters of their own souls. They live by their own standards even though enjoying each other intensely (p. 154).

Cognition and Self-Actualization

Habits are at once necessary and dangerous, useful and harmful. They save us time, effort, and thought, but at a big expense. They are the prime weapon of adaptation and yet they hinder adaptation. They are problem solutions and yet in the long run they are the antonyms of fresh, creative thinking, of solutions to new problems. They tend to replace in a lazy way, true, fresh, attending, perceiving, learning, and thinking (Argyris, 1962). The four factors mentioned--natural laziness or simian reluctance, fondness for assimilating the new to the old, tradition and success--have contributed to keep our thought undeveloped. The periods of intense intellectual ferment and tradition-shattering thinking have been extraordinarily rare within the historical period. The thinking of Plato and Aristotle sufficed from the Greek times to the Renaissance, and the thinking of Galileo and Descartes at the Renaissance furnished natural science with a stock of fundamental notions that have needed little revision until recent times. Thus, during the most of the intervening times, thinking has chiefly been a process of working out bad habits (p. 32).

Self-actualized people do not use habits because they are lazy. Their use is to simplify life so that more important activities can be undertaken. When a person cannot find his socks and shoes because they are hidden someplace in the room, it behooves him to establish some habits which will make life more efficient. This habit-making activity can be as simple as this, or more elaborate, depending upon the action the person needs to perform. Self-actualized people avoid habitualizing their thinking in order to avoid placing themselves into a closet which doesn't have any light in it and eventually no way out. They prefer to leave their lives, their activities, their cognitive processes open-ended (deBono, 1985).

Thinking is the technique through which human beings create something new. This implies that thinking must be revolutionary in the sense of occasionally conflicting with what has already been concluded. If it conflicts with the intellectual "status quo" it is then the opposite of habit, or memory, or what the person has already learned. By definition, it contradicts what habits produce for us; namely, orderliness, efficiency, and maintenance of the status quo. True, free thinking breaks our habits, our patterns of living, our cultural taboos. Creative thinking is exemplified by boldness, daring, and courage. No creative thinking activity of mankind ever involved the warming up of yesterday's leftovers (deBono, 1987).

There is then a certain contrast between classifying experiences and appreciating them, between using them and enjoying them, between cognizing them in one way and creatively using them in another. All writers on the mystic and religious experiences emphasized this as few technical psychologists have. Huxley (1944) said: "As the individual grows up, his knowledge becomes more conceptual and systematic in form, and its factual, utilitarian content is enormously increased. But these gains are offset by a certain deterioration in the quality of immediate apprehension, a blunting and a loss of intuitive power" (p. vii).

Unless the individual can break away from fossilizing his thinking, he will be subject to: 1) having only stereotypical problems or in failing to perceive new ones; (2) using only stereotyped and rote habits and techniques for solving these problems; (3) having in advance of all life's problems, sets of ready made, cut and dried solutions and answers. These three tendencies add up to an almost complete guarantee against creativeness and inventiveness (Argyris, 1965). "The essence of life," he wrote, "is to be found in the frustrations of established order. The Universe refuses the deadening influence of complete conformity. And yet in its refusal, it passes toward novel order as a primary requisite for important experience. We have to explain the aim at forms of order, and the aim at novelty of order, and the measure of success, and the measure of failure" (p. 119).

This is not to say that holistic thinking is not used in creative thinking. It is, and the point is that it is used only in a different way. This results in intrinsic learning and the person becomes the person he or she is to become potentially (Maslow, 1946). The bold thinker must be able to break the "Einstellung," to be able to be free of the past, of habit, expectation, learning, custom, and convention, and to be free of anxiety whenever venturing out of the safe and familiar harbor (Rand, 1943).

Self-actualized people avoid such rubrics, such stereotypical thinking. Their desire is to be free of convention, of the common, ordinary, mundane, rhetorically backward. They choose to live on the edge, making up the rules of life as they go along. As Picasso said, "Every act of creation is first, an act of destruction." It is not that they want to "burn the mother down," but they want to experience some new and wondrous ways of living their lives. They maximize their potential by asking, "What is it that I want to achieve? How can I achieve it?" Then they go about the business of achieving what they want to without worrying about the conventions of society. This is not a simple undertaking. All civilizations, societies, communities, families, and friends, conspire to stop this process. What appears to be new, exciting, and different, frightens even the most foresighted individuals in society. The die is cast. The battle lines are often drawn. If the person wants to pursue his or her self-actualization, then there will need to be a break with tradition, habit, habitualizing thinking. People who walk beyond the sidewalk of society without regard for conventional wisdom and thinking and can accept the "slings and arrows" of outrageous public opinion, will succeed in their own unique and inimitable way. Their motivation is to fulfill the highest of human needs. They refuse to accept less because to do so is to limit them. Contrary to common sense, they function beyond the realm of what is common, maintaining that common sense is not very common for if it were so prevalent, it would be possessed by more people. They eventually succeed in their own way, much like James Joyce (1950) did when he completed **Finnegan's Wake**, a novel few understood but all admired. They speak poetically of the future, and live their daily lives walking to the beat of pentameters and not hollow footsteps. Theirs is a noble, yet divergent existence beyond reasonability.

Occidental Purposefulness and Oriental Beingness

Western culture rests on the Judao-Christian theology. The United States particularly is dominated by the Puritan Work Ethic which stresses work, struggle, striving, soberness, earnestness, and above all, purposefulness (Allport, 1933). American psychology is overpragmatic, over-Puritan, and overpurposeful. From the point of view of values, there is a preoccupation with means to the exclusion of concern with ends. The culmination of this perspective may be found in explicit form in Dewey's **Theory of Valuation** (1939) in which the possibility of ends is in effect denied; they are themselves only means to other means, to other means..., etc. In his later writings, Dewey did accept the existence of ends.

Causality theory is a suitable tool for the life of achievement and technological accomplishment, but is completely useless for the life that stresses intensive perfection, aesthetic experience, contemplation of ultimate values, enjoyment, meditativeness, connoisseurship, and self-actualization.

Motivation is not synonymous with determination. Although it was Freud (1920) who originally confounded the two concepts, his mistake has been so widely followed by psychoanalysts that they now automatically look for motives only no matter what change occurs.

The study of self-actualizing people makes it clear there is a necessity for distinguishing between their motivational life and that of more average people. They clearly live a self-fulfilling, value-enjoying, self-perfecting life, rather than seeking for the basic need gratification that the average citizen lacks. Self-actualization is the coming to full development and actuality of the potentialities of the organism, and is more akin to growth and maturation than it is to habit formation or association via reward. Behavior is means rather than end. Behavior gets things done in the world. Ends are frequently subjective experiences of satisfaction. Without reference to the fact that most instrumental behaviors have human worth only because they bring about these subjective end-experiences, the behavior itself often becomes scientifically senseless (Young,

1941). Behaviorism may be understood better if it is seen as one cultural expression of the general Puritan striving and achieving point of view already mentioned. This implies that to its various other failings must now be added ethnocentrism.

The creation of art may be relatively motivated when it seeks to communicate, to arouse emotion, to show, to do something to another person, or it may be relatively unmotivated when it is expressive rather than communicative, intrapersonal rather than interpersonal. What is important for the sophisticated person is the question of the aesthetic experience. It is so rich and valuable an experience for so many people that they will simply scorn or sneer at any psychological that denies or neglects it. Even the aesthetic perception may be seen as relatively unmotivated by comparison with ordinary cognitions.

A useful jumping-off point for thinking about just being, is the analysis of the concept of waiting. For instance, the cat in the sun does not wait any more than a tree waits. Waiting implies wasted, unappreciated time that is empty of significance for the organism. It is a by-product of a too exclusively means-oriented attitude toward life. It is seen as a stupid, inefficient, wasteful response. Travel is an excellent example of the way in which a piece of time can be either enjoyed as an end experience or completely wasted. Education is another instance, as are interpersonal relations in general.

There is an old Taoist belief that says, "Sit still long enough in one place and the whole world will pass you by." Imagine the Average American standing still long enough to even let his family pass him by. No, we are not prone to standing, sitting, or even walking slowly from one point to another. Our crowded freeways are an example of this

(Ironically, the question is, why do we call them freeways?). For the use-oriented, purposeful, need-reducing kind of person time is wasted that achieves nothing and serves no purpose. In Tao belief, "Time you enjoy wasting is not wasted time." And, "Some things that are not necessary may yet be essential." An excellent illustration of the way American culture is unable to take its end experiences straight may be seen in strolling, canoeing, golfing, and other pastimes. These activities are extolled because they get people into the open, close to nature, out into the sunshine, or into beautiful surroundings. In essence, these are ways in which what should be unmotivated end activities and end experiences are thrown into a purposeful, achieving, pragmatic framework in order to appease the Occidental conscience. Imagine any ardent golfer not keeping score or talking about his round after it is over. He will replay the entire experience, analyze every shot, and delimit the game into a scientific exercise. This is the American way. It is also anti-self-actualizing.

The mystic experience, the experience of awe, of delight, of wonder, of mystery, and of admiration are all subjectively rich experiences of the same passive, aesthetic ones that beat their way in upon the organism, flooding it as music does. These are end experiences, ultimate rather than instrumental, changing the outside world not at all. All this is true for leisure as well if properly defined (Pieper, 1964).

As for the basic life pleasure, any ailing or dyspeptic or nauseated person can testify to the reality of that most ultimate biological pleasure that is an automatic, unsought for, unmotivated by-product of being, fully alive and healthy.

In self-actualized people, the truth is simply perceived without effort, rather than struggled for or sought after. The fact that in most experiments, motivation of some sort is necessary before problems can be solved. This might be a function of the triviality or arbitrariness of the problems rather than proof that all thinking must be motivated. In the good life lived by healthy people, thinking, like perceiving, is spontaneous and passive reception or production. It is unmotivated, effortless. It is a happy expression of the nature and existence of the organism. They let things happen rather than make them happen, like the flower makes perfume or the tree makes an apple.

Normally Healthy People and Their Values

Drucker (1939) presented the thesis that western Europe, since the beginning of Christianity, was dominated by four successive ideas regarding how individual happiness and welfare were achieved. Each of these held up a certain type of man as ideal, and assumed that if only this ideal were followed, individual happiness and welfare would result.

1. Middle Ages: Spiritual man.

2. Renaissance: Intellectual man.

3. Capitalism: Economic man.

4. Fascism: Heroic man.

Drucker maintained that all these concepts have failed and are now giving way to the fifth concept, psychologically, healthy, or "natural" man. What will this new man, woman, child be like? The following describe this individual:

1. Humans possess an essentially, individual nature; some skeleton of psychological structure that may be treated analogously with physical nature; some needs, capacities, and tendencies that are in part genetically based; some needs are on their face good or neutral rather than evil.

2.   Full health and normal, desirable development
      consist in actualizing this nature, in fulfilling
      these potentialities, and in developing into
      maturity along the lines that this hidden, covert,
      dimly seen essential nature dictates, growing
      from within rather than being shaped from
      without.

3.   Most psychopathology results from the denial or
      the frustration or the twisting of man's essential
      nature (p. 124).

Drucker's contention was similar to Aristotle's that the
"good life consists in living in accordance with the true nature
of man." Maslow (1970) contended that Aristotle did not
know enough about the true nature of man to propose this.
All that Aristotle could do in describing this essential nature
was to look around him and observe people, and build a
picture of the good man in his own culture and in that
particular period of time. His work lacked external validity.
The essential difference between the Aristotelian Theory and
the modern conceptions of Goldstein, Fromm, Horney,
Rogers, Buhler, May, Grof, Dabrowski, Murray, Sutich,
Bugental, Allport, Frankl, Murphy, Maslow, Robbins, and
others is that we can seen not only the surface, not only the
actualities, but the potentialities as well. Modern
psychologists can better understand what lies hidden in man,
what lies suppressed, neglected, and unseen. They can
further judge the possibilities, the potentialities, and the
highest possible achievements available to humans. Maslow
(1970) concluded that, "history has practically always sold
human nature short" (p. 271).

Current thinking regarding normal human
development accepts that self-realization cannot be attained
by intellect or rationality alone. Aristotle maintained that

reason the highest quality in humans. Now, rationality, along with emotionality, and the conative, wishing, and driving side of human nature are all present in the healthy, normal, human being. Fromm (1947) said, "Reason has become a guard set to watch its prisoner, human nature, and thus both sides of human nature, reason, and emotion, were crippled as captives." The realization of self occurs with acts of thinking as well as the active expression of emotional and instinctual capacities as well.

Maslow (1970) contended:

WHAT WE CAN BE = WHAT WE OUGHT TO BE

To be empirical, the "ought" is out of place. What **ought** a cat to become? The answer to this question is ludicrous for the cat. Likewise, it is for the human being as well. In a single moment of time, it is possible to distinguish between what a human **is** and what he or she **could be**. Humans are comprised of layers of behaviors, attitudes, beliefs, thoughts, emotions, and all coexist, even though they may contradict each other at any given time. Understanding and accepting that an individual may behave badly and may yet be loving deep down inside provides the individual with hope for improvement in the species of mankind.

Man's inherent design or inner nature are his anatomy and physiology, and also his most basic needs, yearnings, and psychological capacities. This inner nature is usually not obvious and easily seen, but is hidden and unfilled, weak rather than strong. Maslow (1970) maintained that four separate lines of evidence existed to support this position.

1. Frustration of these needs and capacities is psychopathogenic;

2. Their gratification is healthy-character-fostering as neurotic need gratifications are not;

3.	They spontaneously show themselves as choices under free conditions;

4.	They can be directly studied in relatively healthy people (p. 274).

Giving gratification to neurotic needs does not breed health as does gratification of basic inherent needs. Giving a power hungry neurotic power seeker all the power he wants does not make him less neurotic, nor is it possible to satisfy his neurotic need for power. However much he is fed he still remains hungry. It makes little difference for ultimate health whether a neurotic need be gratified or frustrated. It is different with basic needs like safety and love. Their gratification breeds health, their satiation is possible, their frustration does breed sickness (Maslow, 1965).

Practically all healthy adults have led loving lives. They love and are loved. As adults, they are now loving people. Finally, they need love less than the average person, apparently because they already have enough. Just as an organism needs salt in order to attain health and avoid illness, so to does it need love for the same reason. The organism is so designed that it needs salt, and love, in the same way an automobile is designed that it needs gas and oil (p. 296).

Healthy adults, in a psychological utopia, would tend to be more Taoistic, nonintrusive, and basic need-gratifying. They would be far less controlling, violent, contemptuous, or overbearing than humans are in general. Under such conditions, the deepest layers of human nature would emerge with ease. Inquiry into the effect of culture on health indicates that individuals can be healthier than the culture in which they grow and live. This is possible because of the ability of the healthy human being to be detached from his or her surroundings, which is to say that humans live by inner laws rather than by outer pressures (p. 298).

Healthy individuals are not usually externally visible. They are not marked off by unusual clothes, or manners, or behavior. It is an inner freedom that they have. They are independent of the approval and disapproval from other people, and seek self-approval instead. Tolerance and freedom of taste and opinion seem to be the key necessities (p. 280).

The neglect of higher needs and neglect of the differences between lower and higher needs dooms people to disappointment when wanting continues even after a need is gratified. In the healthy person, gratification produces no cessation of desire, but after a temporary period of contentment, substitution of higher desires and higher frustration levels along with the same old restlessness and dissatisfaction.

Sex is customarily discussed as if it were a problem. The preoccupation with the dangers of sex has obscured the obvious that it can be or should be a very enjoyable pastime and possibly also very profoundly therapeutic and educational one (p. 286).

Thinking in the healthiest people is not of the Dewey type, stimulated by some upsetting problem or nuisance, and disappearing when the problem is solved. It is spontaneous, sportive, and pleasurable, and is often emitted or produced without effort. Thinking is not always directed, organized, motivated, or goal-bent. Fantasy, dreaming, symbolism, unconscious thinking, infantile, emotional, thinking, psychoanalytic free association, are all productive in their own way. Healthy people come to many of their conclusions and decisions with the aid of their own innate common sense.

The behavior of a healthy person is less determined by anxiety, fear, insecurity, guilt, shame, and more by truth, logic, justice, reality, fairness, fitness, beauty, rightness, and morals. The subject for a positive psychology is the study of psychological health, aesthetic health, value health, physical health, and the like. What produces the socially desirable characteristics of kindliness, social conscience, helpfulness, neighborliness, identification, tolerance, friendliness, desire for justice, righteous indignation? The taste, values, attitudes, and the choices of self-actualizing people are to a great extent on an intrinsic and reality-determined basis, rather than on a relative and extrinsic basis. They live within stable system of values and not a robot world of limited values or none at all. Frustration level and frustration tolerance may be higher in self-actualized people (p. 293).

Maslow prompted psychologists in the last half of the 20th Century to consider new and better ways to view human beings, and especially, human motivation. His hierarchy is well-known. People in casual conversation talk about fulfilling their needs, and becoming self-actualized. Just as Freud's work precipitated a flurry of work by his followers, Maslow's hypotheses also caused psychologists to use his work as a springboard to new and unique explanations for what motivates people. But unlike Freud, his work created the proliferation of self-help programs that sprung up in the past thirty years. What made his work exciting to many followers was his emphasis on the positive, forward-thinking approach to viewing human beings. He eschewed neuroses, and promoted healthy living, healthy human behaviors, attitudes, and beliefs.

Up until Darwin, the major forces thought to cause behavioral arousal, direction, and persistence were seen to be physical for the animal and both physical and spiritual for the human being. This division stemmed from a number of philosophical and theological considerations developed over a period of more than two thousand years. The understanding of the motivational processes of animals could be done in a mechanistic fashion. The motivational process of the human was controlled by his physiological needs and desires, his knowledge, and his will. The conscious, human will served to balance and control gluttonous, physical, and sexual desires of the body.

Maslow's contribution to the inquiry into what motivates human beings was moving away from animal experimentation and moving toward the observation of healthy, self-actualized individuals in an attempt to observe directly what characteristics make them so unique. He made startling discoveries that made the world of psychology and sociology dig deeper into the nature of man and his motives. Until his theories were published in 1954, most motivational theories were limited to causal relationships with little validity in the real world. Maslow admitted that his work lacked some clinical and experimental validity, and yet he did not foresee any difficulty in translating his theories.

More research needs to be conducted into Maslow's theories in order to further validate them.

11. INTRINSIC AND EXTRINSIC MOTIVATION

Intrinsic motivation is the performance of a task purely for the joy of doing it. There is no reward except in accomplishing the task the individual set out to complete. Conversely, extrinsic motivation is the performance of a task for some external reward. The most common form in a capitalist society is money. What separates these two forms of motivation is that one is difficult to measure because it is difficult to determine for each individual what it is that motivates him or her. External motivating factors are often visible and tangible.

Current research into both areas reveals that individuals can be motivated both intrinsically and extrinsically, separately, and sometimes, simultaneously. Some individuals are more prone to accept extrinsic motivational factors than others. This does not mean that they shun external factors; they just prefer internal ones.

Is one more important or powerful than the other? There is no definitive answer to this question. However, intrinsic motivation prompts individuals to strive for goals in the absence of any discernable reward. Externally motivated individuals, in the absence of rewards may become unmotivated unless there is some hope for measurable reward in the end.

What does current research into these two unique forms of motivation reveal? The following are an overview of some findings in business, industry, and education. Intrinsic and extrinsic motivation are reviewed simultaneously because both capture the essence of this aspect of human motivation.

Boggiano and Barrett (1992) examined whether extrinsic children were more depressed than intrinsic children and whether this effect was more pronounced for girls than for boys. Sixty seven female and 60 male 3rd-grade children completed self-report measures assessing motivational orientation (MO) and depressive symptoms. Subjects with an extrinsic MO (i.e., subjects who performed a task for approval or fear of evaluation) were more depressed than those with an intrinsic MO. Significant gender differences show that girls were more extrinsic than boys and thus more susceptible to helplessness and depression.

Fair and Silvestri (1992) reviewed literature on the effects of rewards, competition, and success/failure on intrinsic motivation. Data indicated that intrinsically motivated individuals with an internal desire to excel are superior in both quality and quantity of task performance to externally motivated performers. Studies of children and adults credited praise and positive verbal affirmations with increasing internal motivation, and external rewards and punishment with decreasing internal motivation. Although the sexes were not significantly different in internal motivation, they appeared to vary in their approach to competitive situations. They suggested ways to increase motivation including the need for enough praise and positive affirmation at every step of the way through a process to enhance both children and adults to achieve at maximum levels.

Boggiano and Katz (1991) tested the hypothesis that the importance of adult approval and feedback for females relative to males would render girls of elementary school age more likely to develop an extrinsic orientation in comparison to boys. Using Harter's (1981) Scale of Intrinsic versus Extrinsic Motivation, the data supported the hypothesis for Study 1 in which 107 girls and 106 boys in 4th-6th grades participated. Because of the assumed differential importance of controlling feedback from adults for females relative to males, a second study examined 64, 9-11 yr old girls' and boys' preference for challenge as a function of adult controlling feedback and children's motivational orientation. The data supported the hypothesis that girls relative to boys show differential preferences for challenge, depending on the presence and type of adult feedback and motivational orientation in girls.

Enzle, Roggeveen, and Look (1991) hypothesized that ambiguous behavior standards coupled with self-administration of rewards would reduce intrinsic motivation whereas clear standards coupled with self-administration of rewards would maintain high preexisting levels of intrinsic motivation. Fifty four university students participated in a study comprised of a 2 (ambiguous vs unambiguous standards) by 2 (self- vs other-administered reward) factorial design and unrewarded control group. Results supported their predictions. Behavior standard clarity was a critical determinant of whether self-administration protected or undermined initially high intrinsic motivation.

Lawler, Armstead, and Patton (1991) attempted to integrate the concept of the type A behavior pattern with the research on intrinsic motivation. The hypothesis that type A behaviors focus attention on extrinsic rather than intrinsic motivation was tested by measuring type A behavior and motivational orientation in 95 male college students. Results were consistent with the hypothesis. Type A subjects were also unaffected by instructions designed to increase intrinsic motivation, whereas type B subjects were highly sensitive to such instructions. These data provide an explanation for the paradoxical effect of type A behavior in males (i.e., success accompanied by feelings of dissatisfaction). They suggested more research needed to be conducted to determine what motivated type B individuals.

Wiersma (1991) found contrasting predictions from expectancy valence and cognitive evaluation theories while testing his hypothesis when testing using a 2 * 2 factorial design in which intrinsic and extrinsic rewards were manipulated. Several relevant factors were also considered, namely type of extrinsic reward, measure of intrinsic motivation, and use of moderator variables (e.g., higher order need strength). Ninety four undergraduates worked on either an interesting or boring task for a low or high extrinsic reward. The primary measure of intrinsic motivation was the subjects' return rate to a second experimental session. Results supported the expectancy valence hypothesis that intrinsic and contingent extrinsic rewards have an additive effect on motivation. Both types of rewards showed significant main effects. There were no significant moderator effects found.

Koestner et al (1991) examined whether motives as assessed from fantasy (seen as implicit needs) were primarily aroused by factors intrinsic to the process of performing an activity, whereas motives obtained through self-report inventories (seen as self-attributed needs) were aroused by social factors that were extrinsic to the process of performing an activity (e.g., the way in which a task is presented by an experimenter). In Experiment 1, with 71 college students, performance on a memory task depended on the interaction of subjects' self-reported motive for achievement with achievement-arousing instructions, whereas performance on a word-finding puzzle depended on the interaction of subjects' fantasy need for achievement with the puzzle's level of intrinsic challenge. Experiment 2, with 54 college students, generalized these findings to the power domain.

Sakurai (1990) examined the self-evaluative motivation (SEM) model proposed by Sakurai (1990), using four kinds of extrinsic rewards (verbal, token, verbal and token, and feedback only) among 110 6th graders. According to the SEM model, experimental groups should select more difficult tasks (receiving no rewards or feedback) than the control group because they have higher feelings of competence. The token, verbal and token, and control groups should select more dissimilar tasks than verbal and feedback groups because the former groups have little feeling of self-determination. In the experiment, subjects were assigned lucky-puzzle tasks and given extrinsic rewards or feedback. They were asked which task they wanted to try among four kinds of tasks that were similar or dissimilar to the previous task and easy or difficult. Results supported the behavioral predictions of the SEM model.

Tripathi (1991) studied the effects of contingency and timing of reward on intrinsic motivation for subsequent task performance in 65 undergraduates. After completing the mandatory problem session, subjects spent a significantly greater amount of free-activity time solving puzzles under performance-contingent reward conditions, followed by task-contingent reward with feedback, and task-contingent reward conditions, respectively. Performance on problem-solving tasks during a free-activity period yielded a significant effect of reward contingency, implying greater intrinsic motivation under performance-contingent reward, followed by task-contingent reward with feedback, and task-contingent reward conditions, respectively. The effect of timing of reward was not significant. The roles of challenge and competence information facilitated intrinsic motivation for task performance.

Diaz-Soto (1989) examined differences in home environment, motivational orientation, and relationships among the home environment and the motivational orientation of 28 higher and 29 lower achieving 5th- and 6th-grade Puerto Rican children. The relative weights of the variables and their ability to predict achievement were examined via a post-hoc multiple regression analysis. Home interviews were conducted using the Family Environment Schedule (Marjoribanks, 1979) and a scale of intrinsic vs extrinsic orientation. Gender differences were also noted. Family involvement accounted for a significant amount of variance with regard to achievement. Home environment differed for the higher and lower achievers' family, with parental aspirations higher for higher achievers. Motivational orientation differed, with higher achievers adopting a more intrinsic orientation and lower achievers adopting a more extrinsic orientation.

Rummel and Feinberg (1990) examined the effect of motivational orientation on intrinsic motivation among 40 females. Use of the Jonckheere Test of Order (A. R. Jonckheere, 1954) suggested that the detrimental effect of extrinsic rewards on intrinsic motivation might be explained within the reinforcement paradigm. Intrinsically motivated subjects who received intrinsic rewards showed the highest amount of intrinsic motivation as assessed by free time on the Soma puzzle. Extrinsically motivated subjects receiving intrinsic rewards showed the lowest amount of free time. Rewarding intrinsically motivated subjects negatively affected their motivation while just the opposite was true for the extrinsically motivated ones.

Mawhinney (1990) described cognitive and behavior analytic approaches to the study of intrinsic and extrinsic reward effects and considered the implications of differences in these approaches for future study and application. A critique of the research design and data analysis techniques used in Deci's (1971, 1972; Deci and R. M. Ryan, 1985) Deci-type paradigm was presented. A behavioral model of intrinsic reinforcement for use by organizational behavior managers was also described. Evidence contradicting the Deci-type theory indicated that people who are most highly intrinsically motivated by a task are least likely to exhibit any post-extrinsic reinforcement decrement to intrinsic motivation.

Flora (1990) proposed that the use of contingent, "extrinsic" reinforcement undermines the rate at which "intrinsically interesting" behaviors occur. A review of the literature suggested that environmental stimuli control the rates of behaviors rather than interest intrinsic to the organism. Reduced rates of behavior typically attributed to the undermining of intrinsic interest are more objectively accounted for by environmental stimuli functions, including instructional control and by Herrnstein's (1970) matching law. When the hypothetical version of intrinsic motivation is contrasted with a physiological version, the hypothetical version makes the opposite prediction of every effect that occurs. Recommendations based on the concept of undermining intrinsic interest are flawed and possibly dangerous, he believed and suggested that extrinsic motivating factors should be removed from the intrinsically motivated behavioral situation or event.

Dickinson (1989) wrote that extrinsic consequences have been criticized on the grounds that they decrease intrinsic motivation or internally initiated behavior. Two popular rationales for this criticism, Lepper's (1981) overjustification hypothesis and Deci and Ryan's (1985) motivational theory, were reviewed, and the criticism was then redefined behaviorally. Intrinsically controlled behavior was defined as behavior maintained by response-produced reinforcers. Empirical support for the decrease in the reinforcing value of stimuli caused by extrinsic reinforcement was presented, and possible explanations for the phenomenon were offered. The effect was transient and not likely to occur at all if extrinsic rewards are reinforcing, noncompetitive, based on reasonable performance standards, and delivered repetitively.

Dolke and Srivastava (1988) investigated whether the job attitudes of satisfaction, involvement, and intrinsic motivation were conceptually distinct and empirically independent variables, using questionnaire responses from 200 clerical and 118 technical textile mill workers in India. Results provided fairly strong evidence for treating the three variables as separate attitudes. Findings appeared to be generalizable cross-culturally and they were similar to those obtained by Lawler and Hall (1970) with research scientists and Cummings and Bigelow (1968) with blue-collar workers.

Anderson and Rodin (1989) studied 50 undergraduates who received cues supporting different causality prior to answering a set of brain-teasers on a computer terminal. Results indicated that mild negative feedback increased intrinsic motivation (IM) when it was associated with environmental cues signaling self-determination. Subjects who were given mild negative feedback but who had a choice of problems to solve, no expectation of evaluation, and private discussion of scores, retained as much (or more) IM as subjects given positive feedback under the same conditions. Subjects in controlling contexts showed less IM.

Feldman and Weitz (1988) suggested that a variety of individual, job-related, and organizational factors influence whether employees reach career plateaus. Career plateaus were associated with (1) individual skills, (2) individual needs and values, (3) lack of intrinsic motivation, (4) lack of extrinsic rewards, (5) stress and burnout, and (6) slow organizational growth. They reported that to motivate employees managers must plan strategies to increase individual skills, understand needs and values, support intrinsic motivational patterns, provide extrinsic rewards to those who need them, and increase organizational growth so that employees can strive to fulfill the challenge of promotions being offered by the company.

Deci (1987) suggested that excitement as well competence and self-determination underlie intrinsically motivated behavior. He argued that excitement (which is an emotion) belongs in a different class of concepts from competence and self-determination (which are needs). He also suggested that several recent studies (e.g., Baumeister and Tice, 1985) have added confusion to the intrinsic motivation literature by focusing on paradigms (rather than theories) and operations (rather than constructs). If intrinsically motivated individuals are to be supported, he wrote, then organizations must begin to accept that they exist, and create an environment in which intrinsically motivated individuals can fully develop.

Tang et al (1987) examined the performance of 131 undergraduates, classified as either high or low in self-esteem, on an anagram-solving task labeled as difficult or easy. In the first work period, subjects in the easy condition set higher goals than subjects in the difficult condition. High self-esteem subjects in the easy condition solved more anagrams than those in the difficult condition. In the second period, high self-esteem subjects in the easy condition set higher goals than those in the difficult condition. In the free-choice period, low self-esteem subjects in the easy condition spent significantly less time on the anagram-solving task than did the average of the other groups. The combination of low self-esteem and an easy label led to the lowest level of intrinsic motivation.

Cellar and Wade (1988) studied the effects of behavior modeling (intrinsically vs. extrinsically motivated model) and a symbolic rehearsal intervention (presence vs. absence) on intrinsic motivation, task satisfaction, and script-related recognition. A 2 * 2 factorial design was used with 80 male undergraduates as subjects. As predicted, the motivational orientation of the model affected behavioral measures of intrinsic motivation and script-related recognition. It did not affect self-report measures of interest or task satisfaction. Contrary to expectations, the symbolic rehearsal intervention had no effect on these variables. Regression analysis revealed that the intrinsic script-recognition measures explained incremental variance in intrinsic motivation beyond measures of locus of causality and perceived self-competence, suggesting that a script-processing model may add to existing intrinsic motivation theory.

Reeve et al (1987) conducted two experiments with 107 female and 78 male undergraduates that examined individual differences of need for achievement, anxiety, locus of control, and gender to determine their intervening role in intrinsic motivational processes following objective competence information. Subjects were either allowed to win or were made to lose a puzzle-solving contest against a same-gender confederate with the success/failure experience serving as the objective source of competence information. In experiment I, the outcome, locus of control, and the resultant achievement motivation * outcome interaction predicted level of intrinsic motivation, thereby substantiating the claim that individual differences are important in the prediction of intrinsic motivation. Experiment II showed that the need for achievement affected level of intrinsic motivation through the high achievers' favorably biased performance expectancy and heightened positive affect, and, after losing, through both favorable actual and perceived performance relative to low achievers.

Kohn (1987) discussed research on intrinsic task motivation, defined as the delight in doing something for its own sake, and examined the relation between creativity, external rewards, and motivation. The work of Amabile (1986) suggested that the intrinsic motivation principle of creativity questions the behaviorists' assumption that any activity is more likely to occur if it is rewarded. Environmental factors that aid creativity (e.g., encouragement, autonomy) were reviewed and added as variables that enhance the intrinsic motivation to be creative, some of which were a trust, encouragement, acceptance of divergent thinking, and support for nonconformity.

Most studies of intrinsic motivation under reward and evaluative contingencies have used social comparison criteria to evaluate subjects' performance. In those studies evaluation tended to reduce intrinsic interest. Harackiewicz et al (1987) contrasted normative evaluation against a more task-focused evaluation of subjects' performance on an interesting word game and examined the role of achievement motivation in moderating reactions to performance evaluation. Focus differences were implemented under conditions of performance-contingent reward, anticipated evaluation, and control conditions in which subjects received performance feedback at task conclusion. They predicted that evaluation would reduce interest relative to reward and feedback control groups under a normative focus but not under a task focus and also that a process of competence valuation (Harackiewicz & Manderlink, 1984) would mediate the effects of reward and achievement on interest, especially in normative conditions. The data conformed to these expectations with one exception: evaluation under a task focus increased intrinsic interest. These results were interpreted in the context of a general model that considers the separate effects of situational contingencies, personality factors, performance and motivational processes, and evaluative outcomes on intrinsic motivation.

Sinha (1986) administered questionnaires designed to assess job satisfaction, intrinsic motivation, work values, and job involvement to 60 government and 50 private-enterprise employees in India. Questionnaires included items from instruments developed by Lawler and Hall (1970), Blood (1969), the Institute for Social Research at the University of Michigan, and U. N. Agarwala (1976). Analysis of data obtained from the 60 completed questionnaires was accomplished using t -tests and correlations. Quality dimensions correlated positively with satisfaction, and some differences could be detected between private and government workers.

Orpen (1986) administered the Pay Satisfaction Questionnaire (Heneman and Schwab; see PA, Vol 73:20996) to 47 managers from a variety of industries. Subjects also completed measures of job involvement, work satisfaction, and internal motivation, and provided self-ratings of performance, absenteeism, and turnover. Results showed that only 2 of the 24 correlations between these outcomes and satisfaction with pay level, raises, benefits, and structure were significant, those between pay level and motivation and pay level and involvement. Results suggested that subjects pay was unrelated to job attitudes that lead to high motivation and performance.

Shalley et al (1987) examined the possibility that participative goal-setting methods combined with goal difficulty and expected external evaluation to affect intrinsic motivation, using 96 male undergraduates. Subjects were assigned to one of eight experimental conditions. Results indicated that only the method of setting goals had an effect on intrinsic motivation. Subjects who were assigned goals exhibited significantly higher levels of intrinsic motivation than those who participated in setting goals.

In this experiment, Koestner et al (1987) examined the relation between content of praise, type of involvement, and intrinsic motivation. College students were introduced to a hidden-figure task in either an ego-involving (i.e., test-like) or task-involving (i.e., game-like) manner and then received either ability-focused, effort-focused, or no praise for their performance. As predicted, task involvement increased intrinsic motivation relative to ego involvement, and ability praise increased intrinsic motivation relative to effort praise or no praise. Furthermore, praise and involvement interacted so that subjects who received effort praise were relatively more intrinsically motivated under task-involving than ego-involving conditions, whereas those who received ability praise were relatively more motivated under ego-involving than task-involving conditions. The higher levels of intrinsic motivation were accompanied by a choice of a higher level of challenge and better performance at a related but more complex task. Finally, a significant Sex * Praise interaction was found, reflecting that women tended to display more intrinsic motivation in the no-praise condition than in the two praise conditions, whereas men showed the reverse pattern.

Reeves et al (1986) asked undergraduates in experiment I to list favorite and least favorite activities and report the predominant affective experience underlying the activities. Results showed that, in a majority of cases, subjects reported excitement rather than either competence or autonomy as the feeling most associated with their favorite activities. In experiment II, the traditional intrinsic motivation paradigm was used with 31 undergraduates. Results showed that excitement had a significant, positive association with each of four indices of intrinsic motivation. It was concluded that excitement functioned as a third reward in intrinsic motivational processes.

Sugihara (1985) investigated the hypothesis that test anxiety (TA) was one of the main factors undermining intrinsic motivation. Two hundred and sixty three male undergraduates with high and low TA were assigned to a test or no-test condition. Subjects engaged in solving puzzles in both conditions. Only those in the test condition were told that the task was a kind of intelligence test. The intrinsic motivation of high-TA subjects did not differ significantly between conditions, while that of low-TA's were significantly lower in the test than in the no-test condition. In order to foster intrinsic motivation in learners, text anxiety needs to be diminished so that motivation is enhanced.

Sansone (1986) examined whether competence information is the feedback feature that affects intrinsic motivation and whether perceived competence is the process responsible in two studies in which 174 undergraduates compared competence feedback with meaningful task feedback. In study one, positive competence feedback and task feedback were manipulated independently. Findings indicated that although positive feedback resulted in the highest level of perceived competence, both positive and task feedback enhanced interest individually. In study two, an ego-involvement manipulation emphasized competence prior to task engagement. Path-analytic techniques were used to identify two processes that mediated the effects of positive, negative, and task feedback on interest: perceived competence and personal valuation. Results indicated that perceived competence enhanced enjoyment only when performance quality was stressed by the ego-involvement manipulation. When competence was not made salient, subsequent interest depended more on the degree the individual personally valued involvement. Both studies indicated that competence information can affect both perceived competence and personal valuation. Feeling competent itself enhanced intrinsic motivation only if attaining competence was a primary goal of the task.

To summarize the research cited above, intrinsic motivation was sometimes negatively influenced by extrinsic factors. If intrinsic motivation is characterized by the pure delight in doing something just for the joy of doing it, then extrinsic factors, when added to the motivation equation, can inhibit the individual from intrinsically pursuing his or her goal. The intrinsic/extrinsic motivational theories do not possess the same amount of complexity that some of the earlier ones reviewed do. They are important because they provide some manner of describing what motivates individuals who appear to be doing something just for the pleasure of doing it. This was a departure from the earlier researchers who theorized that causal relationships existed between **D** (drive) and motivation. Finally, intrinsically motivated individuals comprise a unique group of individuals. Under normal circumstances, extrinsic motivation seems to be more commonplace because it is something which can be seen, heard, and measured. Intrinsic motivation is difficult to measure because it is centered in the affective rather than the cognitive or psychomotor domains.

12. THE WORK ETHIC AS A MOTIVATION FACTOR

The American Constitution is a secular document, shaped by secular political philosophers, but sanctified with popular attitudes derived from religion, especially from the Protestant Work Ethic (PWE). This impulse imbued the Constitution with the idea of "bettering oneself" and of economic progress, and made it the cornerstone of an American civil religion that drives the economic, political, educational, industrial, and religious activities of a nation. The PWE is a term that is used to describe this principle in America (Kristol, 1987). Overman (1983) supported this position. He researched a collection of commentary on work and play, including sources spanning some three centuries of American history. He noted that the work ethic, in its various forms and shades, perceptibly provided the leitmotif for the American experience in work and play, and was an earlier form of defining work ethic and other types of motivation.

In order to better understand the PWE as a motivating factor in humans, research in many diverse areas conducted by educators, businesses, and politicians describes how it enhanced the development of the civilization as we know it, and the way individuals fit into it via their own work ethic.

Early Americans were credited with holding the Protestant work ethic, a set of work-related beliefs involving the traits of industriousness, individualism, asceticism, community involvement, and an overall valuing of work as the most worthwhile way to spend one's time. Tang (1988) found that the American work ethic today is not the same as it was in early America. In order to examine whether the American work ethic today was undergoing a significant change, he studied the major characteristics of individuals who endorsed the Protestant work ethic. He investigated the relationships between the Protestant work ethic and some demographic variables in a sample of 689 subjects in the middle Tennessee area. Subjects completed a 25-page questionnaire which included the Mirels-Garrett Protestant Work Ethic Scale and items measuring selected demographic variables. The results revealed that the PWE endorsement was positively related to Republican Party identification and negatively related to age, educational level, employment status, annual income level, and marital status.

Hedges (1983) examined indicators that have been used to assess job commitment: statistical series on absence from work; quits; working part time by choice (phenomena generally associated with weak commitment); and multiple job-holding and overtime (often associated with strong commitment). He found that the those who worked full time correlated highest with self-esteem, and a propensity to achieve to the fullest, and those who worked part-time were significantly lower on self-esteem and fulfillment.

Super (1982) presented a model for examining the role of work. He discovered the importance of the work ethic and the role of work in meeting people's needs. His results identified in the Work Importance Study identified commitment, participation, and knowledge as the basic motivating components of work or other life-career roles.

Stanton (1983) reviewed the decline in productivity and motivation, theories of work motivation, and changes in the work ethic and work attitudes in America. He recommended the revitalization of five essentials of sound management: recruitment and selection, training and development, performance appraisal, supervision, and compensation. He that the PWE was not dead, but dormant, due to the evolutionary changes taking place in the economic environment in America and the world.

Grant (1982) examined possible reasons for declining employee motivation and found these: greater instability and diversity of values; more guaranteed rewards; inability of rewards to satisfy emerging needs; disappearing work ethic; reduced costs of failure; rising income and progressive taxation; more group production and problem solving; decreased employee loyalty; less supervisory power; shorter time perspectives. He concluded that the PWE was not in demise but was shifting its form and beginning to evolve into a 21st century structure.

Maywood (1982) cited three studies which indicated that today's worker is searching for personal significance in his/her job. He considered this problem: what is the role of vocational education in helping our society to build and maintain a reasonable work ethic? No definitive answers were discovered, but he indicated that the work ethic was not in decline but in flux in America for a variety of reasons like the changing economic structure, the advent of the information age, and new and better forms of management which have facilitated participatory management in the organizations worldwide.

In Canada, Maguire (1982) described the development of an instrument to measure high school students' opinions toward the world of work and the results of administering the 75-item questionnaire to 1,035 students in Alberta. He showed their opinions supportive of the traditional PWE. He indicated his results tended to be consistent with those presented in literature.

Thomas (1982) surveyed 50 graduate students in rehabilitation counseling regarding their attitudes toward the Protestant Work Ethic (PWE). He found the students more likely to endorse those aspects of the PWE reflecting the intrinsic value of work were those dealing with the condition of people rather than those concerned with their earnings, social status, and advancement for themselves.

In studying the effects of money and status on motivation, Tang and Gilbert (1992) found that money significantly impacted peoples' motivation, behavior, and performance. Their study was conducted to further validate and explore the Money Ethic Scale (MES), an instrument developed to examine the meaning of money, in a sample of mental health workers in Tennessee. It examined mental health workers' (N=155) attitudes toward money, as measured by the MES, exploring how those attitudes related to demographic, personality, and organizational variables. The results of separate step-wise multiple regression analyses for the six factors of the MES scale (money is good, money is evil, money represents achievement, money represents respect, money represents freedom/power, and "I budget my money carefully") showed that males tended to feel more strongly that money represented respect, freedom, and power than did females. The respect factor was also associated with a Type A personality. Respondents who endorsed the Protestant Work Ethic tended to think that money represented achievement and that money was good. Respondents who claimed that they budgeted their money carefully tended to have high self-esteem, Type A personalities, be older, have low organizational stress, and have low incomes. Intrinsic job satisfaction was related to the attitude that money represented freedom and power, whereas extrinsic job satisfaction was related to the notion than money is not evil.

In a separate study, Tang (1991) suggested that the PWE is a multidimensional concept. The concept of PWE has been examined in many different samples and societies. Little research has been done concerning the factor structure of the PWE scale in a Chinese sample. He examined the factor structure of the PWE scale in a sample of medical students (N=115) in Taiwan. The 19-item PWE scale was administered to these students. The subjects were asked to rate each item on a 7-point scale. Data were subjected to principal components factor analysis. Four factors were identified as PWE behaviors: hard work, internal motive, asceticism, and leisure. The factors of hard work, asceticism, and leisure were closely related to three factors revealed in Furham's previous research. However, factors such as religion and morality and independence from others were not found in this study. This was caused by the fact that seven measures of the PWE were used in Furham's research and only one measure was used in this study. He reported that future research may compare the endorsement of the PWE in different groups and populations in the same or different cultures or societies.

One answer to rekindling the PWE in the American work place was presented by Levitan (1991). He explored the role of public jobs programs in the U.S. economy from the 1930s to the present. He postulated that jobs programs are necessary because they serve four separate but overlapping needs: alleviating joblessness, hardship, and poverty; helping the economy emerge from recession; providing jobs to able-bodied welfare recipients; and producing needed services that otherwise are neglected. He showed that jobs programs are necessary even in good economic times so that disadvantaged persons can secure employment that the private sector will not give them. He also recounted the problems of previous jobs programs, such as insufficient management, too-rigid selection processes, unworkable compensation formulas, and substitution of federal funds for local government funds, and suggests ways to avoid these pitfalls. Finally, he recommended job programs for the 1990s as a way to work out of recession, have needed work done, and promote the work ethic as a motivating factor to improve the productivity and self-esteem of American workers.

Relating school learning to work can make adolescents take school more seriously. Hamilton (1990) proposed that the one mission of schools is to prepare the young to assume work roles. Schools were used to teach basic academic material and a work ethic that were equally applicable to a wide range of occupations. He cited John Dewey who argued that preparation cannot be effective unless it simultaneously addresses immediate needs and interests. Although U.S. vocational schools teach job-related knowledge and skills in preparation for employment, the German Berufsschule teaches the same lessons after employment has started. The Berufsschule comes about as close as possible to integrating instruction in job-related knowledge and skills at school and work. Schools should engage young people in critical reflection on their work experience as a means of fostering their ability to understand work places as sociotechnical systems and, using that understanding, to act constructively to improve them and to improve their positions in them. This is very different from seeking the direct transfer of job-specific knowledge and skills, general academic subjects, or of problem-solving strategies. Principles for practicing this integration include the following: (1) reflection is a process of discovery; (2) learners become action-researchers; (3) the social impact of technology should be examined; and (4) journals, critical incidents, and literature are useful aids to reflection.

Poole (1989) developed an instructional activities guide intended to integrate a comprehensive program of instruction in employability skills into the local K-12 curriculum in Wisconsin. The nine employability skills taught were the work ethic, commitment, communication, interpersonal relationships, responsibility, job-seeking and job-getting, reasoning and problem-solving, health and safety habits, and personal attributes. The beginning sections explained the document's background, listed the employability skills and associated competencies, and introduced the instructional activities. Instructional activities followed for each employability skill. In each case, the activities appeared in groups for lower elementary, upper elementary, middle-junior high, and high school students. For each activity, materials, procedures, evaluation methods, and enrichment activities were suggested. Materials such as checklists, sample letters to employers, sample reward stickers, interview questions, puzzles, mystery game clues, patterns to be duplicated, and assignment logs were included.

While concerns grow regarding the possible "decline" of America's traditional work ethic, there is a growing interest in Japanese economic successes and their work ethic. Engel (1985) compared the work ethics of American and Japanese men. A questionnaire was designed to measure values related to America's "Protestant work ethics" and to traditional Japanese work ethics. Work Ethic Questionnaires were distributed to samples of 220 American and 368 Japanese employed men. T-test comparisons of groups resulted in significant differences on 29 of 34 work ethic items. American men were found to place a higher value on individualism, independence, and self-sufficiency, and tended to believe that education and hard work lead to success. Japanese men were found to place a higher value on group involvement, loyalty to employer and country, and large over small organizations;

and tended to agree with many of the values that have been termed "Puritan" or "Protestant work ethic" in America. Results were discussed in terms of American and Japanese cultural traditions and change. The data provided evidence that "Protestant ethics" are still strong in America, while some aspects of traditional Japanese work ethics may be changing. More culturally diverse research was needed, the author concluded.

In order to prepare the future generation of young people for work in the 21st century, new strategies will need to be implemented by the educational establishment. Some of these are presented in the following studies.

According to a survey of 148 small business employers conducted by McCoy and Reed (1991), schools should teach youngsters basic math, reading, listening, speaking, and writing skills, along with specialized skills needed for technology, business, public service, personal service, health, and consumer occupations. Schools should also teach good grooming, healthy habits, and the old-fashioned work ethic, meaning that hard work will pay dividends in the end.

McCracken (1990) supported this position. He maintained that although values are the most important outcome for vocational education, they are often considered as extraneous. The curriculum should teach and practice the work ethic, further egalitarianism and educational unity, and develop an awareness of global issues.

Etlinger (1990) found that minority participation in the work force, and by extension in vocational education, was becoming increasingly important to the economic welfare of the United States. He described the need for focusing on minority issues and concerns in vocational education related to programs, students, staff, and research. He recommended the development of role models, funding, and curriculum, and teaching the work ethic as part of a regeneration of values that could lead to success in the future for an entire generation of disenfranchised minority youths.

Miller (1989) hypothesized that vocational ethics instruction is education that develops an enabling work ethic. Small group discussion activities can promote values assessment for ethical choices, mediation skills for conflict resolution, and reasoning skills for recognizing and solving ethical problems. Miller and Coady (1988) presented a model for teaching vocational ethics and helping students develop an enabling work ethic. It concentrated on teaching two main types of skills: ethical reasoning skills and mediation skills. The format of instruction included presenting and discussing ethical problems as related to the work place. They maintained that conscious teaching of the work ethic could instill in the next generation the same ethic.

Naylor (1988) completed extensive research into this issue. She proposed a new concept, vocational ethics, as an extension of what appeared to be the demise of the PWE. She found that many studies described how employers have traditionally agreed on the behaviors and attitudes they expect from employees and on the security and benefits that they are willing to provide in return. Various factors, including rapid technological advancement and increased foreign competition, have changed this. Today's workers generally have less job security than their predecessors. Different employers require different attitudes and behaviors from their employees. These changes made it necessary for vocational and career educators to revise their approach to preparing students to enter and function in the world of work.

This revised approach, which has come to be known as vocational ethics, is intended to (1) provide students with a framework for recognizing and resolving internal and external ethical conflicts and (2) give students the opportunity to develop an enabling work ethic. Vocational ethics instruction is centered around two main topics: ethical reasoning skills and mediation skills (assertiveness, emphatic listening, principled negotiation, and risk taking).

Studies conducted in the 1970s (Maywood 1982) provided evidence that employers have traditionally agreed on the behaviors and attitudes they expect from employees and the security and benefits that they are willing to provide in return. According to Maywood, employers' rankings of the attributes most desired in employees consistently confirm that the most desirable employee is one who demonstrates the traditionally valued characteristics of reliability, dependability, pride of craftsmanship, and willingness to learn and who derives personal gratification from a job well done. Vocational education has traditionally responded to this need through instruction on appropriate work behaviors and attitudes. An example of this approach is teaching students to exercise integrity and good judgment (maintain and demonstrate confidentiality, loyalty, and honesty), respect property, and follow company rules (follow company policies and procedures and negotiate to resolve conflicts) (Lankard 1987).

The transition from an economy based on local agriculture and manufacturing markets to a global, information-based economy has been accompanied by an increasing orientation toward jobs based on mental rather than physical activity. The following changes have especially profound implications for the work place:

1. In an attempt to meet increasing foreign competition by improving product quality and productivity, management has begun to encourage and, in many cases, require greater worker participation in decisions affecting both the quality of the work environment and the production process. According to Wirth (Miller and Coady 1984), this trend has blurred the traditionally sharp demarcation between labor and management.

2. The accelerating pace of technological advancement has made it much less likely that workers will hold the same job throughout their working lives, and the increasing economic pressures brought to bear by a global economy have made it far less likely that workers will begin and end their working lives at the same organization (Miller and Coady 1984).

3. As organizations adopt different strategies to increase their productivity and improve the quality of their product or service, they adopt the new collaboration-based model of structuring the work place to different degrees. Sometimes an organization will even adopt the model to varying degrees in different facets of its operations. One example cited by Wirth (Miller and Coady 1984) is Anheuser-Busch, which has plants based on both the traditional and collaborative models.

These two emerging trends--the blurring of the traditional sharp demarcations between the rights and responsibilities of labor and management and rapid technological and economic change, have resulted in reduced job security. Jennings stated that "sometimes the economy, the high-tech and service sector-oriented kind of economy of the future, may be healthy as a whole precisely by virtue of an extremely and rapidly fluctuating job market" (Miller and Coady 1984, p. 17). As job security decreases and as job restructuring and career change become more widespread, vocational educators charged with preparing students to enter and function in the world of work must bear the additional responsibility of equipping students with the thinking and negotiating skills necessary to manage their own career development.

A second result of the changes in the work place is that different employers have begun requiring and expecting different attitudes and behaviors from their employees. According to Miller and Coady (1986), as early as 1982, U.S. companies were beginning to differ with regard to the value themes they emphasize; hence their conclusion that students being prepared for the post-industrial work place must be made aware that (1) no one set of values may be assumed to be held in equal value by all organizations at all times and that (2) employers may not be "the single source of guiding work values in all work contexts" (Miller and Coady 1986, p. 5).

To distinguish between work maturity, work ethic, and vocational ethics, the term "work maturity skills" is defined as the set of attitudes and behaviors; punctuality, honesty, dependability, taking pride in one's work that has traditionally been expected of employees (Lankard 1987).

According to Miller and Coady (1986), the term "work ethic" refers to the "beliefs, values, and principles that guide the way individuals interpret and act upon their job rights and responsibilities within the work context at any given time" (p. 5). In his discussion of changing attitudes toward work, Maywood (1982) defined the "Protestant work ethic" as the view that humans have a moral duty to work diligently, regardless of their station in life, and that by doing so they can reap societal regard and the personal reward of knowing that a job has been well done. This Protestant work ethic has, according to Maywood, Jennings, Wirth, and others, largely shaped the traditional approach to teaching students about appropriate work attitudes and behaviors.

Miller and Coady (1986) pointed out that, as innovation, flexibility, and collaborative efforts are accepted on an increasingly wider scale, the way in which many of these values (for example, punctuality) are viewed will differ dramatically from employer to employer. Vocational educators and career counselors will have to focus less on teaching a set of universally accepted skills and values (such as those associated with the PWE) and more on equipping students with the higher-order decision-making and problem-solving skills that they will need to cope with increased individual responsibility for shaping their work environments. In many respects, this shift away from specifics to higher-order and more generalizable skills parallels the movement away from job-specific to transferable skills that is occurring in many vocational programs.

This revised approach to preparing students to enter and function in the world of work has come to be known as "vocational ethics." The use of the word "ethics" here should not be interpreted in its general sense of a theory or system of moral values. The definition of vocational ethics offered by

Jennings, "the rights of a worker as well as the rights that management demands of a worker and what a worker demands reciprocally" (Miller and Coady 1986, p. 67) makes it clear that ethics in this context has a narrower scope that is perhaps closer in meaning to "professional ethics."

Miller and Coady (1986) defined the purpose of vocational ethics as being to (1) provide students with a framework for recognizing and resolving ethical conflicts within themselves, with others, and with their environment in such a way as to promote individual job satisfaction and continuous and productive employment, and (2) give students the opportunity to develop an enabling work ethic (p. 5).

This viewpoint is reinforced by Copa et al. (1985). One of the purposes they identified for vocational education is to "socialize individuals to manage the work aspects of their lives in a way that is to their benefit and that of the larger community" (p. 7-7). Dimensions of this role include the relation of work to community, relation of self to work, and relation of work to other facets of an individual's life.

Miller and Coady outlined strategies and materials for use in teaching vocational ethics and helping students develop more individual responsibility through (1) overt instruction and (2) indirect instruction (also referred to as the "hidden curriculum"). Overt vocational ethics instruction is centered around two main topics: ethical reasoning skills (also termed values assessment criteria) and mediation skills.

Six values assessment criteria provide students with hedecision-making tools needed to make a comprehensive evaluation of options available when they are confronted with an ethical dilemma: reciprocity, consistency, coherence, comprehensiveness, adequacy, and duration. The concept of reciprocity focuses on the impact of a decision on the feelings and situation of those affected by it, consistency refers to the congruity of a decision across situations and over time, coherence focuses on the interrelationship of the people affected by a decision and their relationship to the larger environment, comprehensiveness focuses on the implications of a course of action if everyone in a given environment were to adopt the same course of action, adequacy refers to whether an action satisfactorily addresses all aspects of a given problem, and duration considers the impact of a decision over the long term. The criteria help students consider the direct and indirect consequences of a decision in a manner that is both comprehensive and non-moralizing (Miller and Coady 1986).

The following mediation skills are intended to enable students to implement their decisions successfully.

ASSERTIVENESS. The ability to stand up for one's rights without infringing upon those of others by using such techniques as "I-language"; assertive body language; sensitivity to such factors as location, timing, relationships, and frequency when making assertive statements; giving and appropriately receiving positive and negative feedback; conversation skills such as open-ended questions, self-disclosing statements, and process observation.

EMPATHIC LISTENING. The ability to give verbal feedback demonstrating an understanding of the emotional and intellectual content of others' communications, recognize messages conveyed through facial expressions and body language, recognize when conflicting messages are being conveyed, respond to others with compatible verbal and body language so as to promote interpersonal understanding, empathize with the personal experiences expressed by others, and make statements identifying the feelings and attitudes being expressed by others.

PRINCIPLED NEGOTIATION. The ability to respond to issues rather than the personalities of those involved in negotiations, identify the underlying interests of those involved in the negotiation process, determine the extent to which the stated positions and underlying interests of individuals involved in the negotiation process are compatible, generate a variety of possible solutions to a given problem before entering into the negotiation process, and develop and use objective and fair standards to obtain a negotiated statement.

RISK TAKING. The ability to recognize one's own value hierarchy; estimate one's chances of success or failure relative to a number of courses of action involving risk; understand the influence of deprivation and oversufficiency in relation to one's personal values; understand and predict the consequences of success and failure in a given decision-making process; understand the influence of one's attributions of the causes of one's past failures and successes on future risk-taking behaviors; understand expected outcomes of win-win, win-lose, and lose-lose situations; and understand the influence of group members on one another in making group decisions involving risk (Miller and Coady 1986).

Miller and Coady emphasized that the hidden curriculum, that is, the relationship between the authority figure (teacher) and those charged with carrying out tasks (students), is equally, if not more, important in helping students develop more individual responsibility and the skills required to develop an enabling work ethic. They pointed out the pitfalls of such policies as enforcing mandatory attendance, not enforcing deadlines, emphasizing rote learning, measuring material retained versus concepts mastered, focusing exclusively on "final products" in grading, developing meaningless rewards and punishments, keeping interpersonal contact to a minimum, and settling conflicts in private. Thus, structuring vocational classrooms in accordance with a more democratic, collaborative model provides yet another opportunity for vocational educators to help their students develop a greater appreciation of the consequences of their attitudes and behaviors and thus assume more individual responsibility for them.

Summarizing the research on the PWE, the following characteristics were discovered:

1. PWE was positively related to Republican Party identification and negatively related to age, educational level, employment status, annual income level, and marital status.

2. Those who worked full time correlated highest with self-esteem, and a propensity to achieve to the fullest.

3. Results of the Work Importance Study identified commitment, participation, and knowledge as the basic motivating components of work or other life-career roles.

4.   The PWE was not dead, but dormant, due to the evolutionary changes taking place in the economic environment in America and the world.

5.   The work ethic was not in decline but in flux in America for a variety of reasons.

6.   Students most likely to endorse those aspects of the PWE reflecting the intrinsic value of work were those dealing with the condition of people rather than those concerned with their earnings, social status, and advancement for themselves.

7.   Intrinsic job satisfaction was related to the attitude that money represented freedom/power, whereas extrinsic job satisfaction was related to the notion than money is not evil.

8.   Four factors were identified as PWE behaviors: hard work, internal motive, asceticism, and leisure. The factors of hard work, asceticism, and leisure were also present in those who demonstrated a strong PWE.

9.   In the 1990's schools should engage young people in critical reflection on their work experience as a means of fostering their ability to understand work places as sociotechnical systems and, using that understanding, to act constructively to improve them and to improve their positions in them.

10. The nine employability skills that need to be taught in 1990's schools are the work ethic, commitment, communication, interpersonal relationships, responsibility, job-seeking and job-getting, reasoning and problem-solving, health and safety habits, and personal attributes.

11. Schools should teach youngsters basic math, reading, listening, speaking, and writing skills, along with specialized skills needed for technology, business, public service, personal service, health, and consumer occupations. Schools should also teach good grooming, healthy habits, and the old-fashioned work ethic, meaning that hard work will pay dividends in the end.

12. Vocational ethics instruction supports education that develops an enabling work ethic. Small group discussion activities can promote values assessment for ethical choices, mediation skills for conflict resolution, and reasoning skills for recognizing and solving ethical problems.

13. Vocational ethics instruction (VEI) is centered around two main topics: ethical reasoning skills and mediation skills (assertiveness, emphatic listening, principled negotiation, and risk taking). In its conceptual design, VEI is proposed as one solution to the current dilemma facing the work milieu in America.

13. SELF-MOTIVATION

In the 1970's, 80's, and 90's many different forms of self-motivation techniques emerged. Bandler and Grinder (1979) studied the master therapists in the world and developed a new form of therapy called Neuro-Linguistic Programming (NLP). Neuro was related to the nervous system; linguistic described the language people used to communicate; programming was the manner in which the nervous system and language combine to effect the total human being's interactions with the world. Their work emphasized the ability of the individual to reprogram or create new "anchors" to replace those set into place over a lifetime. They maintained their search was for the "ten minute cure." What was new in NLP was the ability to systematically analyze exceptional people and experiences in such a way that they could become widely available to others through the use of NLP. Using the principles of NLP, it is possible to describe any human activity in a detailed way that allows a person to make many deep and lasting changes quickly and easily. The entire focus of NLP is much too complex to explain here. What it did, however, was lay the foundation for an entire generation of new-age therapies.

One of the most recent is an approach called **The Trigger Technique**, a special kind of conditioned reflex, sometimes called, an anchor (a la Bandler and Grinder). By combining triggers with such mental self-help methods as visualization, relaxation, and mental rehearsal, exceptionally powerful mind programming systems are possible. This is what makes the trigger's technique go much further than just any of the above three individually.

This is the essence of self-help. Once the individual realizes he can make changes in his life that last, he will be motivated to continue to maintain this new life style. Mann extracted the best of NLP, Gestalt Therapy, Transactional Analysis, psychoanalysis, behavior modification, and sensitivity training to develop his own method of self-help, self-improvement, self-motivation.

Mann described how, by using the **Trigger Technique** (TT), an aspiring executive gained all the action-packed motivation she needed to change her career. After three sessions, a war veteran, suffering from recurrent combat nightmares, was able to sleep peacefully again. After two sessions, a salesman dramatically increased his confidence and soon became a star in his company. In just twenty minutes, a timid woman was able to talk to anyone effectively, from an imposing judge to attractive men she wanted to meet. He recounted how his previous work, using old techniques, sometime produced results, but over a period of months, and often, years. He believed he found the simplest, most successful method for increasing self-motivation in individuals.

In order to make triggers available to all his clients, he believed that the technical language and jargon needed to be removed so that the average person could easily understand how to improve his or her own life. He said:

> Triggers does not just give you an intellectual understanding or insight. Exact methods are given to make the specific changes you want. Scientific jargon is stripped off and replaced with clear, everyday language. I include easy to follow, step-by-step instructions and detailed examples of how others have used these techniques to immeasurably enrich their lives (p. 12).

Mann (1987) listed the following techniques as the foundation of his system for self-motivation.

1. Breakthrough Technique #1 - The Trigger - the powerful mental reflex that is the foundation for all mental programming.

2. Breakthrough Technique #2 - The Mental Blueprint - the technique to make mental blueprints of new skills you want to master.

3. Breakthrough Technique #3 - Multichannel Thinking - the mastering of all thinking "channels" and not just one or two that most people get by with.

4. Breakthrough Technique #4 - The Mental Pentagon - the directing of your own personal war against illness, and along with a physician's treatment, to help yourself get well more quickly.

5. Breakthrough Technique #5 - The Inner Power Generator - the breaking of the root of every habit and in particular the inner conflict, not the lack of motivation or willpower.

6. Breakthrough Technique #6 - the ability to hypnotize yourself and program into yourself and into your personality a new set of behaviors, and into your entire nervous system to make the kinds of changes you need to change and achieve success in all aspects of your life (p. 14).

Mann (1987) described self-motivation as an inner idea or emotion that prompts the individual to take action. It is a vital ingredient of success. To achieve goals, the individual must work actively toward achieving them. They can't be wished for. They must be produced. Many goals flounder in the attitude, "I'll do it tomorrow." Mann blunted stated that people who are not motivated to do what is needed are "losers." Losers put off what needs to be done. The dream of dreamers can lead to great achievements. However, the world is not divided between dreamers who only dream and doers, but between dreamers who only dream, and dreamers who also do (p. 3).

In describing the method Mann used to motivate himself to write, he listed the primary triggering mechanisms necessary to effect motivational change in himself.

1.   Decide what outcome you want and then decide you can do this if you decide that it is something you could enjoy this more than anything.

2.   Think of something you already enjoy doing.

3.   Imagine yourself doing what you want to do and doing it well. Think about it intensely, seeing, hearing, and feeling yourself actively engaged in the activity.

4.   At the moment of peak intensity, push down on one part of your body, like your left knee. This creates the trigger, or a one-trial conditioned reflex that can call up these same sensations whenever you press your knee in the same way again.

5.	Imagine yourself doing the activity that you really enjoy doing. See, hear, and feel yourself intensely involved in the activity. At the peak moment of feeling, push down on your left knee. This creates the second trigger.

6.	The next step is to fire off both triggers at one time. This is called, "double-triggering" and produces both sensations simultaneously. After some momentary confusion, the two opposing feelings merged.

7.	Finally, imagine yourself doing the activity you wanted to do in the first place but were having difficulty doing. It is done.

8.	The joy of doing what you originally enjoyed doing erases the old reluctance to doing what you have avoided, just like a new song, when recording on a used tape, erases the old song already recorded on it.

9.	Negative feelings are replaced by positive ones. These positive ones are called, **reservoirs**. The new behavior is called the **target** (p. 5).

A **trigger** is anything that elicits a memory or emotional feeling. There are five kinds of triggers: visual, auditory, sensory, gustatory, and olfactory.

A marriage album is an example of a visual trigger. Couples with a special song have an auditory trigger that arouses emotions and evokes all the other senses in that set of memories. To use a sensory trigger, Mann suggested the individual first recall a memory from his reservoir. When the memory is clear enough for to see, hear, feel, touch, or even taste it in his mind, he merely has to apply pressure to himself. Mann suggested using a knee, squeezing a thumb, making a fist, bringing a hand to your forehead, or blinking the eyes. To awaken these memories, or reservoirs, he just needs to touch himself in the same way again, and those memories will come back instantly. Mann labeled this, "firing the trigger" (p. 7).

If a person does not have a single memory in his reservoir, Mann suggested he can build one by combining a series of memories. Or he can use fantasies. A memory, Mann contended, is only a fantasy that has been defined as "real."

Mann (1987) believed simplicity made the process unique. He attempted to make them as simple as possible so that any person could follow them and achieve a significant change in his or her life. This was in itself a radical change in the way therapy was delivered to those who sought it. Mann outlined the steps necessary to increase self-motivation. They are listed below.

Eight Steps to Increase Your Motivation

1. Decide what your target and reservoir will be.

2. Imagine your reservoir vividly (fishing, dancing, reading, making love, or anything you enjoy doing). Create a trigger by pressing your right knee.

3. Imagine your target, and, when it is clear in your mind, create another trigger by pressing your left knee.

4. Using your intention, be sure your reservoir is definitely stronger than your target.

5.   If necessary, build your reservoir's trigger until it is stronger.

6.   Fire off both triggers at the same time by pressing both knees or whatever you chose as anchors, remembering both your reservoir and your target.

7.   Allow a minute or two for these to combine.

8.   Imagine yourself in the future, performing your target with your newly acquired eagerness. Adjust this image so it feels real. Imagine the rewards of performing your target successfully (p. 9).

In **Reframing**, Bandler and Grinder (1982) described the same process only using different terms. Instead of triggers, they described the pressing of the body as anchoring new experience in a different part. When the two anchors are "collapsed" at the same time, the two merge, just like Mann described, and the negative and positive forces merge and what is left is a new, more powerful anchor (trigger). Imagining performing the process in the future, is called, future pacing. The processes are the same; only the terminology is different.

Motivating yourself using this system can transform life, Mann contended, because inside each human being is a vast reservoir of strengths and abilities to draw upon. Reservoirs are internal human resources like enjoyment, trust, caring, enthusiasm, creativity, and courage. Resources come from human experience when the individual is determined, persistent, courageous, and confident that he can transform his life. Possessing such qualities is what is meant as having "character," "grit," or "the right stuff."

Mann (1987) suggested that if an individual experiences difficulty in making the triggering method work, the following strategies might help.

1. Begin with an easy target. Try something easy until you gain more skill and success. This permits the mastery of skills.

2. Use strong reservoirs. Remember to use a positive reservoir that is stronger than your target.

3. Use three or more channels. Seeing, hearing, feeling, touching, tasting, are all channels of communication to the inner person. (Bandler and Grinder, 1982) refer to these as the VAK, or visual, auditory, and kinaestheic channels).

4. Mentally rehearse. Imagine yourself enjoying your target behavior in the future so that it feels believable to you. Include images of enjoying the rewards of performing your target behavior (p. 17).

Mann (1987) believed the double-triggering method was more sophisticated than merely invoking willpower because it channeled messages to the entire being via the neurotransmitters present in the body (NLP purports the same notion).

Phobias sometimes immobilize individuals to pursue their goals. Mann believed that the double-triggering method along with systematic desensitization, a technique developed by Wolpe and Lazarus (1966) could quickly and easily erase even the deepest ones. He called this "Fast and Easy Triggers" method for erasing, not just eliminating, phobias. He outlined nine steps for erasing individual phobias.

1. Prepare two cards. Label one "Reservoir." On it, list two or three experiences that have the positive feelings you want. These are you assets.

2. On another card, list five incidents during which you suffered fear, starting with the most recent incident and going back in time until you end with the first phobic reaction you can remember. These are your sub-targets.

3. Create a trigger for an asset from your reservoir by pressing your right knee.

4. Create another trigger for your first sub-target by pressing your left knee.

5. Compare your asset to your sub-target. If the asset is stronger, go to number 6. If it is not, build up your trigger with the rest of your reservoir.

6. Double-trigger by pressing both knees at the same time to evoke your reservoir and your first sub-target together.

7. Create a trigger for your second target. Double trigger your reservoir with your second sub-target. Wait until you feel settled.

8. Continue this with all of your sub-targets.

9. See and hear yourself performing your target with the new feelings you have just acquired from your reservoir (p. 29).

Mann wrote that this entire process should take about 20-40 minutes from start to finish. If a person began to feel any return of the phobia later, all he or she would have to do is touch his right knee, or whatever was used for a positive trigger, in the same way done during the session. This will assist in evoking the positive reservoir to help erase the fear. He maintained this was seldom needed because the process works.

Living in the age of "the information explosion" makes it imperative that we learn and retain new information. Although common sense and wisdom are necessary for the minimal amount of success, individuals need to keep well-informed in order to be able to speak effectively and engage in well-rounded conversations. There are small, but no less important, social benefits from being able to learn and recall certain details. For many people, their jobs are constantly being upgraded with new information. Younger people enter the work world with new knowledge, and new technologies are regularly introduced.

Mann (1987) developed a "learning trigger" that could motivate the individual to learn and recall new information.

> Learning is complete only when an individual can recall information when needed. It is a two-phase process: acquisition and retrieval. To achieve this, the learning trigger (LN) is constructed in two phases. First, the reservoir is created. This is usually some powerful emotion that the individual anchors in his body. Then, the target is created, and like in the other double triggering process, they are fired simultaneously, and the learning mood is altered, and the individual places himself into an especially attentive mood motivated to concentrate and learn just as intensely as when he was in the reservoir state of being (p. 69).

An interesting strategy Mann suggested for becoming a phenomenal speller involved creating a repulsive trigger. When an individual sees a misspelled word, he should associate some unpleasant feeling with it like rotten eggs. Then, whenever a word causes an unpleasant feeling, he will think the word is spelled wrong.

Mann (1987) summarized the seven steps for the learning trigger system:

1. Create a trigger for a time you were enjoyably engrossed in some learning activity. Make this trigger stronger than any negative feelings you may have about studying.

2. Fire this learning trigger before each study session.

3. During each study session, fire the trigger and practice visually recalling your material.

4. Similarly, during each study session, fire your trigger and practice recalling your material with your hearing channel.

5. Indulge in fun fantasies about the material you are learning. Use as many channels as you can.

6. Fire your trigger and practice recalling your material with oral and written quizzes.

7. Whenever you need to recall the information studied, fire your trigger (p. 48).

Paying close attention to learning triggers and reviewing material is a small effort to make compared to the real effort it takes took to originally learn the material. A good schedule is to review something right after learning it. After that, to remember something forever, the individual need only review it every year or two. Studies show, according to Mann, that much of what is learned is not lost if not used within three years.

Mann (1987) listed four steps that would enhance an individual's creativity and motivate him to use his mind more powerfully.

1. **Prepare** by gathering information and images. This is the conscious process. Focus on a goal: the problem to be solved or the outcome wanted. Then collect all the relevant data.

2. Begin the **incubation** process. Release conscious hold of the problem. Allow the answer simply to happen. Don't judge the process and free yourself from habitual thoughts and ideas. Daydreams, night dreams, relaxation, self-hypnosis, and bridging exercises are conducive to permitting the unconscious to work out a solution.

3. Wait for **illumination**. Suddenly, seemingly from nowhere, a solution presents itself. With all five channels now strengthened their contributions will be greater.

4. Finally, **verification** takes place. In your imagination, test out whether the solution works and take out any kinks needed to make the idea workable. Again, with five strong channels, the kinks will be more obvious, and ways to take them out more readily forthcoming (p. 68).

Mann believed individual motivation related to physical skills is one of the most difficult to maintain consistently. The mind is often willing to learn but the flesh is weak. He suggested nine steps for improving physical skills learning.

1. Decide what skill you want to practice. Then, use three channels in your imagination.

2. Study your models.

3. From a distance, see and hear yourself performing the desired sport or physical skill.

4. Step into the picture and repeat the scene.

5. If it doesn't feel right, step outside the scene and adjust your actions.

6. Go into the picture again and repeat it.

7. If it feels right, then create a trigger. Discard those behaviors that you cannot make feel right.

8. Imagine yourself in future scenes, firing your trigger and engaging in your new skills.

9. When really playing, concentrate on using your weaker channel (p. 76).

Finally, Mann (1987) described "Gold Medal Winning" trigger methods for self-motivation to improve the quality of an individual's life. He maintained that these mental blueprints can make the difference between living a normal and an extraordinary life.

Step 1. Decide what new behavior you want to learn. Then, using three channels in your imagination, and...

Step 2.   Study your models.

Step 3.   From a distance, see and hear yourself performing the desired behavior.

Step 4.   Step into the picture and repeat the scene.

Step 5.   If it doesn't feel right, step outside the scene and adjust your actions.

Step 6.   Go into the picture again and repeat it.

Step 7.   When it feels right, create a trigger (p. 90).

Step 8.   Imagine yourself in future scenes, firing your trigger and engaging in your new responses.

Though Mann's triggers techniques are simple to follow and certainly unique, he did not indicate in any way his indebtedness to Bandler and Grinder and NLP as the foundation of his work. He called his techniques, "firing triggers" and Bandler and Grinder labeled theirs "collapsing anchors." The processes are both the same. Both used VAK (Visual, Auditory, Kinesthetic) sensory acuity to change the way the individual experiences and interacts with the world. What is exciting about NLP and Triggers is that both methods provide the individual with methods to change behaviors, attitudes, beliefs, phobias, physical limitations, mental physical, and emotional disabilities. What they purport is that the individual is responsible for changing his or her own life. There is no need for professional assistance unless there are some true medical needs involved. Ideally, the individual, if he practices NLP or the trigger techniques, will be able to change those things which are impeding personal motivation.

Robbins (1991) echoed the same strategies in his book, "Personal Power," and in his videos, audio tapes, and infomercials playing on late night television. He denounced the notion that only through intense counseling with a therapist can an individual attain health and well being. Avant-garde psychologists and sociologists, using the dynamic theories created by Bandler and Grinder, are demonstrating in their work that simple and effective ways for individuals to change their lives.

These are but a few of the self-motivation methods available in America today. A comprehensive study of all of them would take more time and space than is available in this text. What is exciting about the possibilities of these new methods for self-motivation is that they remove the hocus-pocus from instituting individual change. They are erasing the idea that change takes years and that there must be some pain involved in effecting it. Rather than continuing to schedule patients for counseling sessions, they expound the adage from the ancient Greeks, "Patient, heal thyself."

With a minimal amount of interpolation, the phrase can be rewritten to, "Human being, motivate thyself."

The possibilities are unlimited and the next decade may see some truly unique technologies and techniques emerge which provide the individual with all the tools he or she needs to dramatically improve the quality of his or her life.

14. WHAT DOES IT ALL MEAN?

If motivation is the force that initiates, directs, and sustains individual or group behavior in order to satisfy a need or to attain a goal, then this inquiry produced volumes of theories, concepts, principles, techniques, and methodologies to understand what it is and how to motivate human beings. What is important to consider is that this force is unique to each individual human being, and there are many forces which drive an individual to struggle to achieve a goal or to fulfill a need.

The early researchers believed there was a causal relationship between what motivated individuals and each attempted to explain how this developed. Their work was primarily based upon animal experimentation, and extrapolating their findings to human beings was suspect. The problem with cause-effect interpretations is that so many variables need to be considered that isolating any one and predicting this one is the factor is almost impossible. What Freud, Hull, and others accomplished was laying the groundwork for later researchers who used direct observation of healthy people to discover what motivates individuals. Their cumulative work remains as an embodiment of the drive on the part of social scientists to raise the level of inquiry into human motivation to a science. Though they did not fully succeed, they did accomplish setting the stage for those to follow.

Maslow's revolutionary work in 1954 broke the clinical and experimental barriers which others before him could not. He was the first to demand that psychologists and sociologists study healthy people and not neurotics. He maintained that motivation was a function of a healthy person's desire to fulfill basic human needs. All human beings were engaged in this lifelong process and only when they died did it end. The progression from safety and survival needs to the final, need for self-actualization created a motivational definition which effectively described the gamut of human endeavors to meet needs. His theory of self-actualization precipitated a flurry of scholarly and clinical work in an attempt to validate his theories. His comprehensive description of the self-actualized person, based upon the research of his contemporaries and his own clinical and real-life observations, provided the Post-War era with a meaningful, easily understood, structure of the basic motivational patterns of normal human beings. He believed that self-actualization was the need all human beings strived to fill. Some individuals would if the environment, their own desire to succeed, and other safety, love, and esteem needs were met simultaneously. A predictable ebb and flow would unfold in anyone's life because of the day to day situations which affected the meeting of the prepotent needs. What is fascinating about the concept of self-actualization is that the potential for all people to meet this need was predicted. Maslow did not discriminate against anyone. He applied his theory generically to all human beings. His 1970 revision of his original theories promoted them even more. He believed that the world in 1970 needed an infusion of self-actualizing information to precipitate more in-depth research into his hypotheses.

Intrinsic motivation, or doing something just for the joy of doing it, is an interesting construct. Unlike extrinsic motivation, which is the motivation to perform a task or achieve a goal with some external reward in mind, intrinsic motivation develops in the affective domain. It is difficult to measure and therefore, sometimes easily misinterpreted by those who are not prone to be motivated by it. Most humans are extrinsically motivated to achieve, produce, or work toward some goal for a reward. This was certainly supported by Maslow. The hungry man or woman will scrounge for food if hunger predominates their lives. If a person feels unsafe, he or she will do anything necessary, including fight and possibly kill, to meet safety needs. What then motivates the artist, the writer, the human with any creative force active in them, to forego eating, sleeping, and other physiological needs just to produce their works of art? This is where intrinsic motivational theory can be applied. There is something more than meeting an extrinsic need that intrinsically motivates creative and other highly productive people. What is this innate factor? Researchers are not sure. Many propositions exist. Some believe that it is the joy of doing alone that motivates individuals. Yet, what causes this joy to surface in one person and not in another? How can intrinsic motivation be created in individuals? How can it be measured, studied, replicated, and instilled in others? Or can it? All these questions remain to be answered in the years ahead.

One of the simplest ways I found in determining what motivated the clients and staff members I work with is to just ask them. What motivates you to do what you are doing, I ask. Interestingly enough, most people experience a difficult time in answering this question. Generally, I find that those individuals are usually low-motivated people. Those who can answer the question without much thought are usually highly motivated people. They need little time because they have pondered this question themselves somewhere in their lives.

If they describe some external reward as their primary motivating factor, naturally, I would assess they are extrinsically motivated individuals. In my work, I find a mix of types. Those who remain in the field for many years not rising in the power structure and making a living but not extravagant wage, are intrinsically motivated individuals.

Another strategy I use to determine what motivates my colleagues is to ask, "If you had the economic security that your present job provides you, what would you be doing with your life today? Would you be here, doing what you are doing, or would you be doing something quite different?" Responses again vary and yet, what I find is that about 50% of the people I work with state they would do just what they are doing right now.

Lastly, when I asked, "If you hit the lottery for a million today, what would you be doing tomorrow?" Now this question usually causes some guffaws. However, once we get beyond its hypothetical condition, many individuals stated they would continue to do just what they are doing. True, they might take more vacations, pay a few bills, and maybe fix up things in their homes that needed fixed. In the end, they wouldn't change their lives all that much. These individuals I would label as being intrinsically motivated to perform the kind of stressful work we do. A few stated they would quit immediately, move to places like Florida or other points south and west, and retire forever and never have to be told what to do again. I have no data to support the 50% projection that divides my colleagues equally between either being extrinsic and intrinsically motivated.

These three questions do provide me with information which makes it easier for me to understand how to motivate an individual to perform up to his or her potential. I admit they are not complicated questions, and in some ways, I believe the reason why people readily answer them is for that very reason.

Extrinsic and intrinsic motivation are interesting but simple constructs and provide some means to understand human motivation. However, they are not comprehensive enough to fully determine what and how to motivate humans, and therefore, the inquiry into what motivates human beings needs to continue.

Since the founding of our nation, the protestant work ethic (PWE) served as one motivating principle that guided the American work force. Until recently, with the advent of the information age and the "Third Wave" (Toffler, 1980), it worked well in describing what motivated humans to achieve at optimal levels. The dynamics occurring in the last five years caused many researchers to wonder if the PWE was slowly dying. What motivated individuals for the past 100 years did not seem to be in effect any longer. New factors were emerging. Where once job security and a good salary were viewed as necessary extrinsic motivating factors for many people, these were no longer as important as certain intrinsic factors that were difficult to measure but certainly in effect. Some researchers believed the PWE was in a transition stage, and would return once these socioeconomic changes leveled off. Others did not think so.

Today, the PWE receives lip-service from industrial age leaders who do not accept the civilization is evolving into a new and quite unique form. In many ways, the conflict described by Toffler (1980) between the supporters of industrial age beliefs and the new information age proponents is one reason the PWE is in such flux. Where once the primary motivating tools used by industrialists was money, status, prestige, in the information age, these were becoming less important. Quality of life, joy in the work being done, and more recreation time and less work related responsibilities all added together to dethrone the PWE as a primary 1990's motivating factor. Loyalty to a company used to be a condition that existed as part of the industrial age. Working for one company throughout an individual's work life disappeared. Currently, the average length of seniority for all companies in America is approximately 2.8 years of service. Projecting this average into a 21 year old individual's work life, he or she could possibly hold at least 10 to 13 different jobs in a life time. True, the PWE might motivate the individual to optimally perform in each job, but I imagine this would be highly unlikely.

The PWE is being ethnically challenged. America is becoming more diverse now than it was in the early 19th Century. In the last decade, Spanish-speaking, hispanic, latinos, East Asian, and other diverse groups of people rapidly immigrated to the western shores and a new "melting" process began. The current dilemma that Haitians are facing is just one more factor which assaults the PWE. As more and more nationalities blend into the culture, there is little hope that a work ethic which was primarily   occidental in nature, would eventually disappear as oriental beliefs and behaviors spread across the land.

Perhaps the PWE is in flux or it is in its demise. As a motivating factor it still drives a part of the American populace to pursue goals and objectives with sometimes careless abandon. In the next decade this construct will face continued challenge as the immigration continues.

The self-motivation theories added another dimension into the inquiry to explain human motivation. Bandler and Grinder laid the foundation for individual self-development by creating neuro-linguistic programming or NLP. They believed that all human experience was anchored in the body, and by accessing these anchors via the VAK (visual, auditory, and kinesthetic) channels, the individual could relocate the anchors and change human experience. Mann (1987) simplified some of their theories and created another self-motivational system he called, Triggers. Though his techniques were not much different than Bandler and Grinder's, he did simplify the techniques an individual could use to motivate himself to change behaviors, attitudes, beliefs, physical health, the ability to learn, phobias, and other barriers which impeded his achieving his potential. Robbins (1985), in describing his philosophy of personal power, added another dimension to the burgeoning self-motivation methodologies.

These theories appeal to many people who resist the notion that they must go to a counselor, therapist, psychiatrist, to effect some change in their lives. The possibility of changing individual behavior without external assistance is not only attractive but for many on a limited budget, economically prudent. Few can afford the cost of professional help. The Robbins tapes cost $49. Bandler and Grinder's four books, all in paperback, can be purchased for less than $75. Mann's text cost only $24. All three would cost less than a couple of hours spent with a licensed psychologist. Given the choice, most individuals, truly desirous of making changes in their lives, would happily purchase them and begin the change process.

As the new century approaches, more self-motivation theories will emerge as the PWE and other more traditional motivating factors decline, and the information age reduces the cost of acquiring and using newly developed theories. What will these theories espouse? Only time will tell, but it is exciting to consider the possibilities of new and more effective methods and practices to motivate human beings to achieve to their potential in a new and different information age.

The complexity of the human being does not permit a simplistic definition for what motivates him to achieve. However, combining all these theories together and taking the best from each can assist the researcher in understanding motivation from many perspectives.

How can these theories help to motivate a person to achieve to his or her potential? This is the essential question that all these theories hoped to achieve.

The environment, **K**, and innate drives do impact the motivation of the individual. If the environment from which the individual comes is rich and supportive, motivation to achieve is almost assured. If there is an innate drive, or an intrinsic motivational factor present in the individual, along with an environment which is like the one described above, then the motivation is further enhanced. This is not enough however, to ensure that motivation will be present because within any type of environment there are motivated and unmotivated individuals. By itself, **K**, does not provide a complete picture of the motivational patterns necessary for the individual to achieve to his potential.

D, drive, and **H**, habit, also support motivational patterns. When the drive is present to achieve at a high level, then the individual is apt to be motivated to excel. Habits which contain drives that are healthy and unsolidified make it possible for the individual to achieve at a higher level.

It would be simplistic to believe that the PWE is enough of a motivating factor to cause individuals to perform to their utmost in work and leisure activities. What is missing in this theory is the translation effect. It contended that from grandfather, to father, and then to son and great grandson, the ethic was passed on like blue eyes and blonde hair. In the late

1980's the PWE lost its impetus. The industrial age was coming to a close and a new age, based upon information management and service industries, was rapidly overwhelming the old guard. Job insecurity, economic downturns and recessions, elimination of the production of hard goods for services, all contributed to the demise of a civilization that founded itself on pride in working hard for extrinsic rewards.

Out of all these theories, only Maslow's transcends time and place. Even though the industrial age is dying and the information age is asserting itself, individuals will continue to strive toward self-actualization as he described it. What makes his hypothesis so appealing is the notion that the individual is in a dynamic state of change. When survival needs are met, their prepotency is eliminated and then safety needs become dominant. Once these are satisfied, then the next level of needs are sought, and this continues until the need for self-actualization is fulfilled. In any type of civilization, his theory fits.

In the agrarian age, farmers sought to grow crops and eliminate the need to live a nomadic existence. The self-actualized farmer was the individual who not only produced enough goods for himself and his family, but was able to produce enough for others. This manifested itself in this century when the American farm worker became the provider for the world. As our industrial complex grew, the American worker produced goods which were the envy of the world.

Our mass production systems were copied by all the first world nations and even to this day, serve as models for nations struggling to industrialize. American workers achieved a level of self-actualization unknown before in the modern world. Though many of the rewards for hard work were extrinsic, there was an inherent pride that caused men and women to proudly display the symbol, **Made in the U.S.A.**.

Now, the information age is spawning a new concept of what work is and how an individual can feel self-actualized within its dynamic structure. Entrepreneurs like Bill Gates and Steve Jobs and Steve Wozniak in the computer industry are just a couple of examples of the new information age leaders who are returning to America a sense of pride in producing state of the art technologies that are affecting the entire global economy as well as communication. Within these hard and software industries, men and women are engaged in creation, reproduction, problem solving, and achieving self-actualization.

These are exciting times in which we live. True, there are problems in all areas of the world that need to be eradicated. Crime in our streets, poverty, homelessness, alcohol and other drug addiction, and health care deficiencies are just a few which affect America. Global issues are more complex and not necessarily under the control of America, the one superpower that still exists, even though we would like to believe we are still able to impact global thinking and behavior. Until nations like Russia and the other Soviet bloc nations solve their economic and social issues, the world will not be safe for democracy. Nations, like people, can self-actualize, yet there is little evidence that these nations and hundreds more like them will achieve this in the near future. Without a supportive environment where survival and safety are present, national self-actualization is unlikely. Inside these nations, there are many people still living at the survival and safety levels and will remain there for what appears to be an entire generation.

All this impacts the inquiry into human motivation? In each nation there are those people who role model self-actualization. In Maslow's (1970) description of the self-actualized individual, he indicated that they are a rare group and tend to seek out one another. If a nation possesses few of this type of individuals, it will be difficult for others to find and model themselves after them. What we find in our search is a group of individuals who are less inhibited, constricted, bound, enculturated than their peers. They are more spontaneous, natural, and human. If there were no choking enculturating forces in our society, we might expect that all human beings would demonstrate this special type of creativeness, ultimately resulting in living fully self-actualized (Anderson, 1959; Maslow, 1958).

This leads to the question, how do the self-motivation strategies of Bandler and Grinder, Mann, Robbins, and a host of other neo-psychologists affect the development of self-actualized individuals? Or do they?

Their work is certainly unique and thought provoking. NLP, Triggers, and Personal Power are new constructs having existed for less than fifteen years. Theirs, like many others, purport they can prompt change faster than most of the other theories, and that is precipitating a whole generation of self-actualizing human beings.

It is too early to tell if this self-motivation movement will impact America or any other First World nation. There are many questions that need to be asked first:

1.   Do the theories really work or are they merely rehashed theories of Freud, Hull, Maslow, and other psychologists and psychiatrists?

2.   How will we measure whether or not they are working?

3.	What kind of outcome would be produced if a predominant part of a nation were to become self-actualized?

4.	How will individuals be motivated to participate in self-motivation programs, workshops, learning experiences?

5.	Who will pay for it?

6.	Is self-actualization something that is worth pursuing or is it merely a psychological construct, a pipe dream that only the "chosen few" will ever achieve, and only for brief periods of time in their lives?

7.	What kind of personality type is most apt to pursue the path toward self-actualization?

All these questions will need to be researched further before any definitive answers will be available for any of us to decide how we may want to change our lives. The last question is the one of greatest interest to me.

Understanding the nature of the self-actualized human being leads me to question whether or not there are certain types of people who are more apt to consistently meet this need throughout their lifetime? How do they achieve this heightened state of being? Is it something intrinsically motivated or is it a function of the need for self-actualization? How does level of learning affect self-actualization? Or does it? What personality type, as measured by Myers-Briggs, is most apt to become a self-actualized person in his or her lifetime?

The inquiry into human motivation is exciting because it attempts to define what is the essence of the prime mover in human behaviors, attitudes, and beliefs. Throughout each period of human endeavor there existed on the sidelines individuals who asked, what motivates those who achieve at the highest levels and realize their own human potential? Perhaps, what is beneath the surface, like the DNA which determines our genetic makeup, is a personality type that is predestined to achieve at a higher level. This would tend to discount the work of the self-motivation theorists who maintain that anyone can motivate him or herself to achieve at the highest levels. In my review of literature, I could not find any research which attempted to answer this question.

Definitions of motivation, how people motivate themselves, factors in motivated and unmotivated behavior, and a plethora of other areas were studied. It would be daring to propose that there are some individuals more likely to become self-actualized individuals based solely on their personality type.

This inquiry would not be an attempt to determine if one person is more prone to self-actualize than another because he or she is a better person. On the contrary, it would attempt to determine if there is any connection between an individual's personality type and his or her tendency to fulfill the need to become self-actualized.

The belief that human beings can heal themselves prompted an entire generation of inquiry into human psychology.

The belief that human beings can motivate themselves subsequently prompted a new movement toward developing self-motivation systems that can elevate ordinary lives into extraordinary ones.

The belief that human beings can achieve a self-actualized existence if they are a certain personality type can add to the body of human knowledge regarding the connection between personality type and the potential for self-actualizing behaviors, attitudes, and beliefs.

As the ancient cartographers once wrote on maps of the known world where the oceans ended and the unknown began, "There, be dragons."

Preparing to tread beyond the scope of current inquiry related to motivation is both exciting and frightening. What if there is no connection between personality type and self-actualization? What if there is no one personality type that achieves any higher or more consistent level of actualization in his or her lifetime? Would the inquiry be meaningless? Would it be a waste of time?

I believe that any inquiry related to human motivation that attempts to further define how it works, for whom it works best, and how it can be used to enhance change in human beings is a worthy pursuit.

Even if "There be dragons" in this search, I accept the challenge to look beyond the horizon.

All that is left to do, is, "Just do it."

REFERENCES

Adams, J.S. (1963). Toward an understanding of inequity. Journal of Abnormal and Social Psychology, 47, 421-436.

Adams, J.S., & Jacobson, P.R. (1964). Effects of wage inequities on work quality. Journal of Abnormal and Social Psychology, 69, 19-25.

Adams, J.S., & Rosenbaum, N.E. (1962). The relationship of worker productivity to cognitive dissonance about wage inequities. Journal of Applied Psychology, 46, 161-164.

Adams, J.C. (1968). The relative effects of various testing atmospheres on spontaneous flexibility, a factor of divergent thinking. Journal of Creative Behavior, 2, 187-193.

Adler, A. (1939). Social interest. New York: Putnam.

Adler, A. (1964). Superiority and social interests: A collection of later writings, H.L. & R.R. Ansbacher (eds.), Evanston, Illinois: Northwestern University Press.

Allport, G., & Vernon, P.E. (1933). Studies in expressive movement. New York: MacMillan.

Allport, G. (1961). Pattern and growth in personality. New York: Holt, Rinehart and Winston.

Amsel, A. (1958). The role of frustrative nonreward in non-continuous reward situations. Psychological Bulletin, 55, 102-119.

Anderson, H.H. (1959). Creativity and its cultivation. New York: Harper & Row.

Anderson, S., & Rodin, J. (1989). Is bad news always bad? Cue and feedback effects on intrinsic motivation. Journal of Applied Social Psychology, 19, 449-467.

Andrews, I.R. (1967). Wage inequity and job performance: An experimental study. Journal of Applied Psychology, 51, 39-49.

Anshen, R. (1942). Science and man. New York: Harcourt, Brace, & World.

Ardrey, R. (1966). The territorial imperative. New York: Atheneum.

Argyris, C. (1962). Interpersonal competence and Organizational effectiveness. Homewood, Illinois: Irwin-Dorsey.

Argyris, C. (1965). Organization and innovation. Homewood, Ill:Irwin.

Aronson, E., & Carlsmith, J.M. (1962). Performance Expectancy as a determinant of actual performance. Journal of Abnormal and Social Psychology, 66, 178-182.

Aronson, E., & Darley, J.M. (1963). The effects of expectancy on volunteering for an unpleasant experience. Journal of Abnormal and Social Psychology, 3, 220-234.

Asch, S.E. (1956). Studies of independence and conformity, Psychology Monograph, 70, 416.

Asch, S.E. (1952). Social psychology. Englewood Cliffs, N.J.: Prentice-Hall.

Atkinson, J.W. (1964). An introduction to motivation. Princeton, N.J.: Van Nostrand.

Atkinson, J.W., & Litwin, G.H. (1960). Achievement motive and test anxiety conceived of as a motive to approach success and to avoid failure. Journal of Personality and Social Psychology, 60, 52-63.

Bandler, R., & Grinder, J. (1979). Frogs into princes. Moab, Utah: Real People Press.

Bandler, R., & Grinder, J. (1982). Reframing. Real People Press.

Bandura, A., Ross, D., & Ross, S.A. (1963). Imitation of film-mediated aggressive models. Journals of Abnormal and Social Psychology, 66, 3-11.

Bandura, A., & Walters, R.H. (1963). Social learning and personality development. New York: Holt, Rinehart & Winston.

Baron, R.M. (1966). Social reinforcement effects as a function of social reinforcement history. Psychological Review, 73, 527-539.

Baron, R.M. (1968). Attitude change through discrepant action: A functional analysis. In A.G. Greenwalt, T.C. Brock, and R.H. Ostrow, (Eds.), Psychological Foundations of Attitudes. New York: Academic Press.

Bem, D.J. (1970). Beliefs, values and human affairs. Wadsworth, Calif.: Brooks-Cole.

Benedict, R. (1970). Synergy in society. American Anthropologist, 15, 15-20.

Berger, S., & Lambert, W.W. (1968). Stimulus-response theory in contemporary social psychology. In G. Lindzey and E. Aronson, (Eds.), Handbook of Social Psychology. Reading, Mass.: Addison-Wesley.

Bergson, H. (1944). Creative evolution. New York: Modern Library.

Berkowitz, L. (1962). Aggression: A social psychological analysis. New York: McGraw-Hill.

Berlyne, D. (1960). Conflict, arousal and curiosity. New York: McGraw-Hill.

Blodgett, H.C. (1929). The effect of the introduction of reward upon the maze performance of rats. University of Colorado Publications in Psychology, 4, 113-134.

Boggiano, A.K., & Katz, D.S. (1991). Mastery motivation in boys and girls: The role of intrinsic versus extrinsic motivation. Sex-Roles, 25, 511-520.

Boggiano, A., & Barrett, M. (1992). Gender differences in depression in children as a function of motivational orientation. Sex-Roles, 26, 11-17.

Brehm, J.W., & Cohen, A.R. (1962). Explorations in cognitive dissonance. New York: John Wiley.

Brookover, W.B., & Thomas, S. (1963-64). Self-concept of ability and school achievement. Sociology of Education, 37, 27-28.

Brown, J.S. (1952). Problems presented by the concept of acquired drive. Current theory in research in motivation. Lincoln, Nebraska: University of Nebraska Press.

Brown, J.S. (1961). The motivation of behavior. New York: McGraw-Hill.

Buhler, C., & Massarik, F. (eds), The course of human life: A study of life goals in the humanistic perspective. New York: Springer.

Burdick, H.A., & Byrnes, A.J. (1958). A test of "strain" toward "symmetry" theories. Journal of Abnormal and Social Psychology, 57, 367-370.

Cannon, W.G., (1932). Wisdom and the body. New York: Norton.

Cellar, D.F., & Wade, K. (1988). Effect of behavioral modeling on intrinsic motivation and script-related recognition. Journal of Applied Psychology, 73, 181-192.

Chenault, J. (1969). A philosophical premise for theory and research, in A. Sutich, (ed.), Readings in Humanistic Psychology, New York: Free Press.

Coch, L., & French, J.R.P. (1948). Overcoming resistance to change. Human Relations, 1, 512-523.

Cofer, C.N., & Appley, M.H. (1964). Motivation: Theory and Research. New York: John Wiley.

Cohen, J. (1969). Secondary motivations. Chicago: Rand McNally.

Collins, B.E., & Guetzkow, H. (1964). A social psychology of group processes for decision making. New York: John Wiley.

Copa, G.; Daines, J.; Ernst, L.; Knight, J.; Leske, G.; Persico, J.; Plihal, J.; and Scholl, S. (1985). Purpose of vocational education in the secondary school. St. Paul: University of Minnesota, 1985.

Cottrell, N., Rittle, B., & Wack, E. (1967). The presence of an audience and list type as joint determinants of performance in paired-associate learning. Journal of Personality, 35, 425-434.

Cowles, J.T. (1937). Food taken as incentives for learning by chimpanzees. Comparative Psychological Monographs, 14,5, Whole No. 71.

Cravens, R.V., & Renner, K.E., (1969). Conditioned hunger. Journal of Experimental Psychology, 81, 312-316.

Cummin, P. (1967). TAT correlates of executive performance. Journal of Applied Psychology, 51, 78-81.

Darley, J.M., & Berscheid, E. (1967). Increased liking as a result of the anticipation of personal contact. Human Relations, 20, 29-40.

D'Arcy, M.C. (1947). The mind and heart of love. New York: Holt, Rinehart and Winston.

Davies, J. (1967). Toward a theory of revolution. American Sociological Review, 27, 5-19.

deCharms, R. (1968). Personal causation: The internal Affective determinant of behavior. New York: Academic Press.

Deci, E.L. (1987). Theories and paradigms, constructs and operations: Intrinsic motivation research is already exciting. Journal of Social Behavior and Personality, 2, 177-185.

Dember, W.N., & Earl, R.W. (1975). Analysis of exploratory, manipulatory and curiosity behaviors. Psychological Review, 64, 91-96.

Dembo, D. (1961). Psychosomatic diagnosis. New York: Oxford University Press.

Denmark, F., & Guttening, M. (1967). Dissonance in the self-concepts and educational concepts of college and non-college oriented women. Journal of Counseling Psychology, 61, 138-40.

Dermer, M., & Berscheid, E. (1972). Self-report of arousal as an indicant of activation level. Behavioral Science, 17, 420-29.

Dewey, J. (1939). Theory of valuation. Chicago: University of Press.

Diaz-Soto, L. (1989). Relationship between home environment and and intrinsic versus extrinsic orientation of higher achieving and lower achieving Puerto Rican children. Educational Research Quarterly, 13, 22-36.

Dolke, A.M., & Srivastava, P.K. (1988). Need satisfaction, job involvement and intrinsic motivation: A factor analytic study. Indian Journal of Applied Psychology, 25, 13-17.

Dollard, J., Doob, L.W., Miller, N.E., Mowrer, O.H., & Sears, R.R. (1939). Frustration and aggression. New Haven: Yale University Press.

Domino, G. (1963). Maternal personality correlates of sons' creativity. Journal of Consulting and Clinical Psychology, 6, 279-290.

Drucker, P.F. (1939). The end of economic man. New York: Day.

Druckman, D. (1967). Dogmatism, renegotiation experience and simulated group representation as determinants of dyadic behavior in a bargaining situation. Journal of Personality and Social Psychology, 6, 279-290.

Eastman, M. (1928). The enjoyment of poetry. New York: Scribners.

Eckhardt, W., & Newcombe, A.G. (1969). Militarism, personality, and other social attitudes. Journal of Conflict Resolutions, 13, 210-219.

Einstein, A., & Infeld, L. (1938). The evolution of physics. New York: Simon and Shuster.

Eisenberger, R. (1972). Explanation of rewards that do not meet tissue needs. Psychological Bulletin, 77, 319-329.

Engel, J.W. (1985). Protestant work ethics: A comparison of American and Japanese working men. Paper presented at the Annual Conference of the American Psychological Association (Los Angeles, CA, August 1985).

Enzle, M.E., Roggeveen, J.P., & Look, S.C. (1991). Self - versus other-reward administration and intrinsic motivation. Journal of Experimental Social Psychology, 25, 468-479.

Erikson, E. (1959). Identity and the life cycle. New York: International Universities Press.

Erlich, H., & Lee, D. (1969). Dogmatism, learning, and resistance to change: A new paradigm. Psychological Bulletin, 71, 249-265.

Etlinger, L.E. (1990). Minority issues in vocational education. Illinois Schools Journal, 70, 37-48.

Fair, E.M., & Silvestri, L. (1992). Effects of rewards, competition and outcome on intrinsic motivation. Journal of Instructional Psychology, 19, 3-8.

Feather, N.T. (1967). An expectancy of success to need achievement and test anxiety. Journal of Personality and Social Psychology, 1, 118-126.

Feshbach, S., & Singer, R.D. (1971). Television and aggression. San Francisco: Jossey-Bass.

Festinger, L.A. (1954). A theory of social comparison processes. Human Relations, 7, 117-140.

Festinger, L.A. (1957). Theory of cognitive dissonance. Evanston, Ill.: Row, Peterson, & Co.

Festinger, L.A., Schacter, S., & Back, K. (1950). Social pressures in informal groups: A study of human factors in housing. New York: Harper & Row.

Fillenbaum, S., & Jackman, A. (1961). Dogmatism and anxiety in relation to problem solving: An extension of Rokeach's results. Journal of Abnormal and Social Psychology, 63, 212-214.

Finkelman, J.M., & Glass, D. (1970). Reappraisal of the relationship between noise and human performance by means of a subsidiary task measure. Journal of Applied Psychology, 54, 211-213.

Fiske, D.W., & Maddi, S.R. (1961). The functions of varied experience. Homewood, Ill.: Dorsey.

Frankl, V. (1969). The will to meaning. New York: World Publishing.

Freud, S. (1933). New introductory lectures on psychoanalysis. New York: W.W. Norton.

Freud, S. (1920). General introduction to psychoanalysis. New York: Boni and Liveright.

Fromm, E. (1941). Escape from freedom. New York: Farrar, Straus & Girioux.

Fromm, E. (1947). Man for himself. New York: Holt, Rinehart and Winston.

Fromm, E. (1964). The heart of man. New York: Harper & Row.

Gailbreath, J., & Cummings, L. (1967). An empirical investigation of the determinants of task performance: Interactive effects between instrumentality-valence and motivational-ability. Organizational Behavior and Human Performance, 2, 237-257.

Georgopoulos, B.S., Mahoney, G.M., & Jones, N.W. (1957). A path-goal approach to productivity. Journal of Applied Psychology, 41, 345-353.

Getzels, J.W., & Jackson, P.W. (1962). Creativity and intelligence. New York: John Wiley.

Glanzer, M. (1953). The role of stimulus satiation in spontaneous alternation. Journal of Experimental Psychology, 45, 387-393.

Glass, D.C. (1972). Theories of consistency and the study of personality. In E.F. Borgatta and W.W. Lambert (Eds.), Handbook of personality theory and research. Chicago: Rand McNally.

Goldfarb, W. (1945). Psychological privation in infancy and subsequent adjustment. American Journal of Orthopsychiatry, 15, 247-255.

Goldstein, K. (1939). The organism. New York: American Book.

Goldstein, K. (1940). Human nature. Cambridge, Mass: Harvard University Press.

Goodman, P., Rose, J.H., & Furcon, J.E. (1970). Comparison of motivational antecedents of the work performance of scientists and engineers. Journal of Applied Psychology, 54, 491-495.

Goodrich, K.P. (1959). Performance in different segments of an instrumental response chain as a function of reinforcement schedule. Journal of Experimental Psychology, 57, 57-63.

Grant, P.C. (1982). Why employee motivation has declined in America. Personnel Journal, 61, 905-909.

Grossman, S.P. (1967). A textbook of physiological psychology. New York: John Wiley.

Guetzkow, H. (1965). The creative person in organizations. In G. Steiner (Ed.), The creative organization. Chicago: University of Chicago Press.

Hackman, J.R., & Porter, L. (1968). Expectancy theory predictions of work effectiveness. Organizational Behavior and Human Performance, 3, 417-426.

Haggard, D.F. (1959). Acquisition of a simple running response as a function of partial and continuous schedules of reinforcement. Psychological Record, 9, 11-18.

Hamilton, S.F. (1990). Linking school learning with learning on the Job. Paper presented at the Annual Meeting of the American Educational Research Association (Boston, MA, April).

Harackiewicz, J.M., Abrahams, S., & Wageman, R. (1987). Performance evaluation and intrinsic motivation: The effects of evaluative focus, rewards, and achievement orientation. Journal of Personality and Social Psychology, 53, 1015-1023.

Harlow, H.F. (1950). Learning motivation by a manipulation drive. Journal of Exceptional Psychology, 40, 228-234.

Harlow, H.F. (1953). Motivation factor in the acquisition of new responses, in R.M. Jones (ed.)., Current theory and research motivation, Lincoln, Neb: University of Nebraska Press.

Harlow, H.F. (1962). The heterosexual affectional system in monkeys. American Psychologist, 17, 1-9.

Harlow, H.F. (1950). Learning motivated by a manipulation drive. Journal of Exceptional Psychology, 40, 228-234.

Harlow, H.F. (1964). Maternal behavior in socially deprived rhesus monkeys. Journal of Abnormal Psychology, 69, 345-355.

Harlow, H.F., & Harlow, M.K., (1965). The affectional systems, in A.M. Schrier, and F. Stollnitz, (eds.) Behavior of Non-Human Primates, Vol 2., New York: Academic Press.

Harlow, H.F., & Harlow, M.K., (1966). Learning to love, American Scientist, 54, 244-272.

Harlow, H.F., & Harlow, M.K., (1962). Social deprivation in monkeys. Scientific American, 207, 136-144.

Harlow, H. (1953). Motivation as a factor in the acquisition of new responses. Organizational Behavior and Human Performances, 3, 24-59.

Harlow, H., & Zimmerman, R. (1959). Affectional responses in the infant monkey. Science, 130, 421-432.

Hedges, J.N. (1983). Job Commitment in America: Is It Waxing or Waning? Monthly Labor Review, 106, 17-24.

Helson, H. (1964). Adaptation-level theory: An experimental and systematic approach to behavior. New York: Harper & Row.

Herzberg, F. (1966). Work and the nature of man. New York: World Publishing.

Hill, W.F. (1968). An attempted clarification of frustration theory. Psychological Review, 75, 173-176.

Hoffman, L.R., Harburg, R.E., & Maier, N.R.F. (1962). Differences and disagreements in creative group problem-solving. Journal of Abnormal and Social Psychology, 75, 206-214.

Holz, W.C., & Azrin, N. (1961). Discriminative properties of punishment. Journal of Experimental Analysis of Behavior, 4, 225-232.

Homans, G. (1950). The human group. New York: Harcourt Brace Jovanovich.

Horney, K. (1937). The neurotic personality of our time. New York: Norton.

Horney, K. (1950). Neurosis and human growth. New York: Norton.

Howells, T.H. (1945). The obsolete dogma of heredity, Psychology Review, 52, 23-34.

Howells, T.H., & Vine, D.O. (1940). The innate differential in social learning. Journal of Abnormal Psychology, 35, 537-548.

Hull, C.L. (1931). Goal attraction and directing ideas conceived as habit phenomena. Psychological Review, 38, 487-506.

Hull, C.L. (1930). Knowledge and purpose as habit mechanisms. Psychological Review, 37, 511-525.

Hull, C.L. (1943). Principles of behavior. New York: Appleton- Century-Croft.

Hull, C.L. (1952). Essentials of behavior. New Haven: Yale University.

Hull, C.L. (1952). A behavior system: An introduction to behavior theory covering the individual organism. New Haven: Yale University Press.

Huxley, A. (1944). The perennial philosophy. New York: Harper & Row.

Isaacson, R., Hutt, M., & Blum, M.L. (1965). The science of behavior. New York: Harper & Row.

James, W. (1943). The varieties of religious experience. New York: Modern Library.

Jordan, N. (1953). Behavioral forces that are a function of attitudes and cognitive organization. Human Relations, 22, 51-66.

Kardiner, A. (1941). The traumatic neuroses of war. New York: Hoeber.

Karsh, E. B. (1962). Effects of number of rewarded trials and intensity of punishment on running speed. Journal of Personality and Social Psychology, 21, 101-111.

Kaufman, H. (1970). Aggression and altruism: A social psychological analysis. New York: Holt, Rinehart & Winston.

Klee, J.B., (1951). Problems of selective behavior. Lincoln, Neb.: University of Nebraska Studies, Series No. 7.

Koestner, R., Weinberger, J., & McClelland, D.C. (1991). Task-intrinsic and social-extrinsic sources of arousal for motives assessed in fantasy and self-report. Journal of Personality, 59, 57-82.

Koestner, R., Zuckerman, M., & Koestner, J. (1987). Praise, involvement, and intrinsic motivation. Journal of Personality, 53, 383-390.

Kogan, N., & Wallach, M. (1967). Risky-shift phenomenon in small decision-making groups: A test of the information exchange hypothesis. Journal of Experimental Social Psychology, 3, 75-84.

Kohler, W. (1938). The place of values in a world of facts. New York: Liveright.

Kohn, A. (1987). Art for art's sake. Psychology Today, 21, 52-57.

Korman, A.K. (1963). Selective perception among first-line supervisors. Personnel Administration, 26, 31-36.

Korman, A.K. (1966). Self-esteem variable in vocational choice. Journal of Applied Psychology, 50, 479-486.

Korman, A.K. (1967). Self-esteem as a moderator of the relationship between self-perceived abilities and vocational choice. Journal of Applied Psychology, 51, 65-67.

Korman, A.K. (1967). Ethical judgments, self-perceptions and vocational choice. 75th Annual Convention, American Psychological Association, Washington, D.C. (b).

Korman, A.K. (1968). Self-esteem, social influence and task performance: Some tests of a theory. Paper presented at the meeting of the American Psychology Association, San Francisco.

Korman, A.K. (1970). Toward an hypothesis of work behavior. Journal of Applied Psychology, 6, 593-613.

Korman, A.K. (1971). Organizational achievement, aggression and creativity: Some suggestions toward an integrated theory. Organizational Behavior and Human Performance, 6, 593-613.

Korman, A.K. (1971). Industrial and organizational psychology. Englewood Cliffs, N.J.: Prentice-Hall.

Korman, A.K. (1974). The psychology of motivation. Englewood Cliffs, N.J.: Prentice-Hall.

Kristol, I. (1987). The spirit of '87. Public-Interest, 86, 3-9.

Kuo, Z.Y. (1921). Cognitive determinants of achieving behavior. Journal of Philosophy, 18, 645-666.

Lacey, J.L. (1950). Individual differences in somatic response patterns. Journal of Comparative and Physiological Psychology, 43, 338-350.

Lankard, B.A. (1987). Practice of ethical behavior: Work maturity skills series competency 4.0. Columbus: The National Center for Research in Vocational Education, The Ohio State University.

Laski, M. (1962). Ecstasy. Bloomington, Ind.: Indiana University Press.

Lawler, E., & Porter, L. (1967). Antecedent attitudes of effective managerial performance. Organizational Behavior and Human Performance, 2, 122-142.

Lawson, R. (1965). Frustration: The study of a concept. New York: Macmillan Company.

Levitan, S.A., & Gallo, F. (1992). Spending to save: Expanding employment opportunities. Occasional Paper 1991-2. George Washington Univ., Washington, D.C. Center for Social Policy Studies.

Levy, D.M. (1934). Experiments on the sucking reflex and social behavior of dogs. American Journal of Orthopsychiatry, 4, 203-234.

Levy, D.M. (1951). The deprived and indulged forms of psycho-pathic personality. American Journal of orthopsychiatry, 21, 250-254.

Lewin, K. (1935). Dynamic theories of personality. New York: McGraw-Hill.

MacLeish, A. (1954). The hamlet of A. MacLeish. New York: Houghton Mifflin.

Maddi, S. (1968). Personalities theories: A comparative appraisal. Homewood, Ill.: Dorsey.

Maguire, T.O. (1982). Opinions of Alberta Students Towards Work. Alberta Journal of Educational Research, 28, 226-47.

Maier, N.R.F., (1949). Frustration: The study of behavior without a goal. New York: McGraw-Hill.

Maier, N.R.F., (1939). Studies of abnormal behavior in the rat. New York: Harper & Row.

Maier, N.R.F., & Hoffman, L.R. (1961). Organization and creative problem solving. Journal of Applied Psychology, 45, 277-280.

Mann, S. (1987). Triggers: A new approach to self-motivation. Englewood Cliffs, N.J.: Prentice-Hall.

Maslow, A.H. (1935). Appetites and hunger in animal motivation. Journal of Comparative Psychology, 20, 75-83.

Maslow, A.H. (1937). The influence of familiarization on preference. Journal of Exceptional Psychology, 2, 9-18.

Maslow, A.H. (1957). Power relationships and patterns of personal development, in A. Kornhauser, (ed.) Problems of Power in American Democracy. Detroit: Wayne University.

Maslow, A.H. (1957). A philosophy of psychology, in J. Fairchild, (ed.), Personal Problems and Psychological Frontiers, New York: Sheridan.

Maslow, A.H. (1958). Emotional blocks to creativity, Journal of Individual Psychology, 14, 51-56.

Maslow, A.H. (1959). New knowledge in human values. New York: Harper & Row.

Maslow, A.H. (1962). Lessons from the peak-experiences. Journal of Humanistic Psychology, 2, 9-18.

Maslow, A.H. (1964). Synergy in the society and in the individual. Journal of Individual Psychology, 20, 153-164.

Maslow, A.H. (1964). Religions, values, and peak experiences. Columbus, Ohio: Ohio State University Press.

Maslow, A.H. (1965). Criteria for judging needs to be instinctoid, in M.R. Jones (ed.), Human Motivation: A Symposium, Lincoln, Nebraska: Univ. Of Nebraska Press.

Maslow, A.H. (1965). Eupsychian management: A journal. Homewood, Illinois: Irwin-Dorsey.

Maslow, A.H. (1967). A theory of metamotivation: The biological rooting of the value-life. Journal of Humanistic Psychology, 7, 93-127.

Maslow, A.H. (1968). Toward a psychology of being, 2nd ed., New York: Van Nostrand Reinhold.

Maslow, A.H. (1969). The farther reaches of human nature. Journal of Transpersonal Psychology, 1, 1-10.

Maslow, A.H. (1969). Theory Z. Journal of Transpersonal Psychology, 1, 31-47.

Maslow, A.H. (1969). Various meanings of transcendence. Journal of Transpersonal Psychology, 1, 55-66.

Mawhinney, T.C. (1990). Decreasing intrinsic "motivation" with extrinsic rewards: Easier said than done. Special Issue: Promoting excellence through performance management. Journal of Organizational Behavior Management, 11, 175-191.

Maywood, A.G. (1982). Vocational education and the work ethic. Canadian Vocational Journal, 18,3, 7-12.

McClelland, D. (1955). Notes for a revised theory of motivation. In D.C. McClelland (Ed.), Studies in motivation. New York: Appleton-Century-Crofts.

McClelland, D. (1961). The achieving society. New York: Van Nostrand Reinhold.

McClelland, D. (1964). The roots of consciousness. New York: Van Nostrand Reinhold.

McClelland, D., & Winter, D.G. (1969). Motivating economic achievement. New York: Free Press.

McCoy, J.A., & Reed, D.F. (1991). Preparing students for the future world of work. NASSP Bulletin, 75, 94-97.

McCracken, J.D. (1990). Rethinking the importance of values as vocational education outcomes. Journal of Vocational Education Research, 15, 1-17.

Meninger, K.A. (1942). Love against hate. New York: Harcourt, Brace & World.

Miller, N.E. (1948). Studies of fear as an acquired drive. Journal of Experimental Psychology, 38, 89-101.

Miller, N.E. (1960). Some motivational effects of brain stimulation and drugs. Federation Proceedings, 19, 846-47.

Miller, N.E., & Dollard, J. (1941). Social learning and imitation. New Haven: Yale University Press.

Miller, P.F., & Coady, W. T., (Eds.). (1984). Report on the proceedings of the conference on the future of the world of work. St. Louis: Washington University.

Miller, P.F., & Coady, W.T. (1986). Vocational ethics: Toward the development of vocational ethics. Springfield, Ill.: Department of Adult, Vocational, and Technical Education.

Miller, P.F., & Coady, W.T. Teaching the ethics of work. Vocational Education Journal, 65, 32-33.

Montgomery, K.C. (1953). Exploratory behavior as a function of "similarity" of stimulus situations. Journal of Comparative and Physiological Psychology, 129-133.

Mowrer, O.H. (1960). Learning theory and behavior. New York: John Wiley.

Murphy, G. (1958). Human potentialities. New York: Harper and Row.

Murray, H.A. (1937). Facts which support the concept of need or drive. Journal of Psychology, 3, 27-42.

Murray, H.A. (1938). Exploration in personality. New York: Oxford University Press.

Naylor, M. (1988). Vocational education and the work ethic in a Changing Workplace. Washington, D.C.: Office of Educational Research and Improvement.

Nisbett, R.E. (1968). Taste, deprivation, and weight determinants of eating behavior. Journal of Comparative and Physiological Psychology, 47, 419-427.

Northrop, F.S.C. (1946). The meeting of east and west. New York: Macmillan.

Northrop, F.S.C. (1946). The logic of the sciences and the humanities. New York: Macmillan.

Olds, J., & Milner, P. (1954). Positive reinforcement produced by electrical stimulation of septal area and other regions in the brain. Journal of Comparative and Physiological Psychology, 47, 419-427.

Orpen, C. (1986). Correlates of pay satisfaction. Psychology Reports, 59, 1205-1206.

Osgood, C.E., & Tannenbaum, P.H. (1955). The principle of congruity in the prediction of attitude change. Psychological Review, 62, 42-55.

Overman, S.J. (1983). Work and Play in America: Three centuries of Commentary. Physical-Educator, 40,4, 184-90.

Overstreet, H. (1949). The mature mind. New York: Norton.

Pallack, M.S., & Pittman, J.S. (1972). General motivational effects of dissonance arousal. Journal of Personality and Social Psychology, 7, 11-20.

Paulus, P.B., & Murdock, P. (1972). Anticipated evaluation and audience presence in the enhancement of dominant responses. Journal of Experimental Social Psychology, 7, 280

Pieper, J. (1964). <u>Leisure, the basis of culture</u>. New York: Pantheon.

Perrin, C.T. (1942). Behavior potentiality as a joint function of the amount of training and the degree of hunger at the time of extinction. <u>Journal of Experimental Psychology</u>, <u>30</u>, 93-113.

Poole, V. (1989). Classroom activities in employability skills for education for employment. Bulletin No. 9479. Wisconsin State Dept. of Public Instruction, Madison.

Rand, A. (1943). <u>The fountainhead</u>. Indianapolis: Bobbs-Merrill.

Reeve, J.M., Olson, B.C., & Cole, S.G. (1987). Intrinsic motivation in competition: The intervening role of four individual differences following objective competence information. <u>Journal of Research in Personality</u>, <u>21</u>, 148-170.

Reeve, J.M., Cole, S.G., & Olson, B.C. (1986). Adding excitement to intrinsic motivation research. <u>Journal of Social Personality</u>, <u>1</u>, 349-363.

Reik, T. (1948). <u>Listening with the third ear</u>. New York: Farrar, Straus, & Giroux.

Reik, T. (1957). <u>Of love and lust</u>. New York: Farrar, Straus, & Giroux.

Restle, F., Andrews, M., & Rokeach, M. (1964). Differences between open and closed minded subjects in learning set and oddity problems. <u>Journal of Abnormal and Social Psychology</u>, <u>5</u>, 416-423.

Riesman, D. (1950). <u>The lonely crowd</u>. New Haven, Conn: Yale University Press.

Robbins, A. (1991). Personal power. New York: Harper & Row.

Rogers, C. (1951). Client centered therapy. Boston, Mass: Houghton Mifflin.

Rogers, C. (1961). On becoming a person. Columbus, Ohio: Merrill.

Rosekraus, F.M. (1967). Choosing to suffer as a consequence of expecting to suffer: A replication. Journal of Personality and Social Psychology, 7, 419-423.

Rummel, A., & Feinberg, R. (1990). Re-evaluation of re-reinforcement? A new look at cognitive evaluation theory. Social Behavior and Personality, 18, 65-79.

Sakurai, S. (1990). The effects of four kinds of extrinsic rewards on intrinsic motivation. Psychologia: An International Journal of Psychology in the Orient, 33, 220-229.

Sansone, C. (1986). A question of competence: The effects of competence and task feedback on intrinsic interest. Journal of Personality and Social Psychology, 51, 918-931.

Sarason, S. (1967). Toward a psychology of change and innovation. American Psychologist, 22, 227-233.

Schacter, S., Goldman, R., & Gordon, A. (1968). Effects of fear food deprivation, and obesity on eating. Journal of Personality and Social Psychology, 70, 231-244.

Schwartz, O., (1951). The psychology of sex. New York: Penguin Books.

Seudfeld, P., & Epstein, Y.A. (1971). Where is the "D" in dissonance? Journal of Personality, 39, 178-188.

Shalley, C.E., Oldham, G.E., & Porac, J.F. (1987). Effects of goal difficulty, goal setting method, and expected external evaluation on intrinsic motivation. Academy of Management Journal, 30, 553-563.

Shaw, M.C. (1968). Underachievement: Useful constructs or mis-leading illusion. Psychology in the Schools, 5, 41-46.

Sheffield, F.D., & Roby, T.B. (1950). Reward value of non-nutritive sweet taste. Journal of Comparative and Physiological Psychology, 44, 3-8.

Sheffield, F.D., Wulf, J.J., & Backer, R. (1951). Reward value of copulation without sex drive reduction. Journal of Comparative and Physiological Psychology, 45, 471-478.

Siegel, P.S., & Milty, J.B. (1969). Secondary reinforcement in relation to shock termination. Psychological Bulletin, 2,7, 12-15.

Sinha, P. (1986). Factors for job satisfaction: For a quality of work. Indian Journal of Behavior, 10, 24-36.

Spence, K.W. (1956). Behavior theory and conditioning. New Haven: Yale University Press.

Spence, K.W. (1960). Behavior theory and learning. New York: Prentice-Hall.

Spergel, I., & Chance, R.L. (1991). National youth gang suppression and intervention program. National Institute on Justice Report, Chicago: University of Chicago Press.

Stagner, R. (1951). Homeostasis as a unifying concept in personality theory. Psychological Review, 58, 5-17.

Stanton, E.S. (1983). A critical reevaluation of motivation, management, and productivity. Journal of Work and Production, 9, 134-145.

Steiner, G. Introduction. In G. Steiner, (Ed.), The creative organization. Chicago: University of Chicago Press.

Strain, G., Unikel, I.P., & Adams, H.E. (1969). Alternation behavior by children from lower socio-economic status groups. Developmental Psychology, 1, 131-133.

Sugihara, Y. (1985). Effects of evaluation by tests on intrinsic motivation: In relation to test anxiety. Japanese Journal of Educational Psychology, 33, 232-236.

Sumner, W.G. (1906). Folkways. New York: Ginn.

Super, D.E. (1982). The relative importance of work: Models and measures for meaningful data. Counseling Psychologist, 10, 95-103.

Suttie, I. (1935). The origins of love and hate. New York: Julian Press.

Sutton, H., & Porter, L.W. (1968). A study of the grapevine in a governmental organization. Personnel Psychology, 21, 223-30.

Tang, T.L., Liu, H., & Vermillion, W.H. (1987). Effects of self-esteem and task labels (difficult vs. easy) on intrinsic motivation, goal setting, and task performance. Journal of General Psychology, 114, 249-262.

Tang, T., & Gilbert, P.R. (1992). Attitudes toward money among mental health workers: Extension and exploration of the money ethic scale. Paper presented at the Annual Meeting of the Southeastern Psychological Association (38th, Knoxville, TN, March 25-28, 1992).

Tang, T. (1991). A factor analytic study of the protestant work ethic. Paper presented at the Annual Convention of the Southwestern Psychological Association (37th, New Orleans, LA, April 11-13, 1991).

Tang, T., & Tzeng, J. (1988). Some demographic correlates of the protestant work ethic. Portions of the paper were presented at the Annual Convention of the Southwestern Psychological Association (34th, Tulsa, OK, April 21-23, 1988).

Thayer, R.E. (1967). Measurement of activation through self-report. Psychological Reports, 20, 663-678.

Thomas, K.R. (1982). The protestant work ethic, disability, and rehabilitation student. Counselor Education and Supervision, 21, 269-73.

Thorndike, E.L. (1940). Human nature and the social order. New York: Macmillan.

Tolman, E.C. (1932). Purposive behavior in animals and men. New York: Appleton-Century-Crofts.

Tolman, E.C. (1955). Principles of performance. Psychological Review, 62, 315-326.

Torcivia, J.M., & Laughlin, P.R. (1968). Dogmatism and concept attainment strategies. Journal of Personality and Social Psychology, 36, 397-400.

Vacchiano, R.B., Strauss, P.S., & Hochman, L. (1969). The open and closed mind: A review of dogmatism. Psychology Bulletin, 71, 271-283.

Van Doren, C. (1936). Three worlds. New York: Harper and Row.

Vernon, M.D. (1969). Human motivation. Cambridge, Mass: Harvard University Press.

Walker, E.L. (1964). Psychological complexity as a basis for a theory of motivation and choice. Nebraska Symposium on Motivation, 12, 47-97.

Wallace, J. (1971). Psychology: A social science. New York: John Wiley.

Walster, E., Aronson, E., & Brown, Z. (1966). Choosing to suffer as a consequence of expecting to suffer: An unexpected finding. Journal of Experimental Social Psychology, 2, 400-406.

Walster, E., Berscheid, E., & Walster, G.W. (1973). New directions in equity research. Journal of Personality and Social Psychology, 25, 151-176.

Weiner, B. (1972). Theories of motivation: From mechanism to cognition. Chicago: Markham Publishing Co.

Weiss, R.F. (1968). An extension of Hullian learning theory to persuasive communication. In A.G. Greenwald, T.C. Brock, & R.H. Ostrow, (Eds.) Psychological Foundations of Attitudes. New York: Academic Press.

Weiss, R.F., & Miller, F.G. (1971). The drive theory of social facilitation. Psychological Review, 78, 249-250.

Wertheimer, M. (1959). Productive thinking, 2nd. ed., New York: Harper & Row.

Wertheimer, M. (1961). The comparative psychology of mental development, 2nd ed.. New York: Harper & Row.

Wertheimer, M. (1961). Some problems in the theory of ethics, in M. Henle (ed.), Documents of Gestalt Psychology, Berkeley, California: University of California Press.

Wheeler, L., & Davis, H. (1967). Social disruption of performance on a DRL schedule. Psychonomic Science, 7, 44-48.

Whitney, R.E. (1971). Agreement and positivity in pleasantness ratings of balanced and unbalanced social situations: A cross cultural study. Journal of Personality and Social Psychology, 66, 68-77.

Wiersma, U.J. (1991). Combined effects of intrinsic and extrinsic rewards motivation. Psychological Reports, 68, 871-882.

Wike, E.L. (1969). Secondary reinforcement: Some research and theoretical issues. In W.J. Arnold (ed.), Nebraska Symposium on Motivation. Lincoln, Nebraska: University of Nebraska Press.

Williams, S.B. (1938). Resistance to extinction as a function of the number of reinforcements. Journal of Experimental Psychology, 23, 506-522.

Wilson, C. (1969). Voyage to a beginning. New York: Crown.

Wilson, C. (1967). Introduction to the new existentialism. Boston: Houghton-Mifflin.

Wolfe, J.B. (1936). Effectiveness of token rewards for chimpanzees. Comparative Psychological Monographs, 12,5, 331-338.

Wolff, W. (1943). The expression of personality. New York: Harper & Row.

Young, P.T. (1948). Appetite, palatability and feeding habit; a critical review. Psychology Bulletin, 45, 289-320.

Young, P.T. (1941). The experimental analysis of appetite, Psychology Bulletin, 38, 129-164.

Zajonc, R.B. (1965). Social facilitation. Science, 149, 269-74.

Zajonc, R.B., Heingartner, W., & Herman, E. (1969). Social enhancement and impairment of performance in the cockroach. Journal of Experimental and Social Psychology, 2, 160-188.

Zajonc, R.B., & Burnstein, E. (1965). The learning of balanced and unbalanced social structures. Journal of Personality, 13, 153-163.

Zajonc, R.B., & Sales, S.M. (1966). Social facilitation of dominant and subdominant responses. Journal of Experimental and Social Psychology, 2, 160-168.

Zajonc, R.B., Forward, J., & Albert, R. (1969). Adaptation of board members to repeated failure or success by their organization. Organizational Behavior and Human Performance, 4, 56-76.

Zander, A., Forward, J., & Albert, R. (1969). Adaptation of board members to repeated failure or success by their organization. Organizational Behavior and Human Performance, 4, 56-76.

Ziller, R.C., Behringer, R., & Goodchilds, J. (1962). Group creativity under conditions of success and failure and variations in group stability. Journal of Applied Psychology, 46, 43-49.

Zimbardo, P.G. (1969). The human choice: Individuation, reason, and order versus deindividuation, impulse, and chaos. Nebraska Symposium on Motivation, 17, 254.

Zimmerman, D.W. (1957). Durable secondary reinforcement: Method and theory. Psychological Review, 64, 373-383.

Zlutnick, S., & Altman, I. (1972). Crowding and human behavior. In J.F. Wohlwill and D.H. Carson (Eds.), Environment and the social sciences: Perspectives and applications, 32, 44-60.